THE PATH TO NO-SELF

THE PATH TO NO-SELF

LIFE AT THE CENTER

BERNADETTE ROBERTS

Foreword by Father Thomas Keating

SHAMBHALA
Boston & London
1985

SHAMBHALA PUBLICATIONS, INC.
314 Dartmouth Street
Boston, Massachusetts 02116

Printed in the United States of America
Distributed in the United States by Random House
and in Canada by Random House of Canada Ltd.

Library of Congress Cataloging in Publication Data
Roberts, Bernadette, 1931-
The path to no-self.
1. Mystical union.   2. Contemplation.   3. Roberts,
Bernadette, 1931-   . I. Title.
BT767.7.R63   1985   248.2'2   84-19340
ISBN 0-87773-306-6
ISBN 0-394-72999-4 (Random House)

Design/Eje Wray
Typesetting/Graphic Composition/Athens GA in Linotron Trump

*To the Cistercian monks of St. Benedict's Monastery
high in the Colorado Rockies.*

CONTENTS

Foreword *ix*
Introduction 3
Phases of the Unitive Life 9
Dichotomy of Experience 15
Phase I 25
Preface to Phase II *49*
Phase II *51*
Phase III *77*
Between Phases III and IV *113*
Phase IV *119*
Phase V *153*
Phase VI *165*
Conclusion *199*

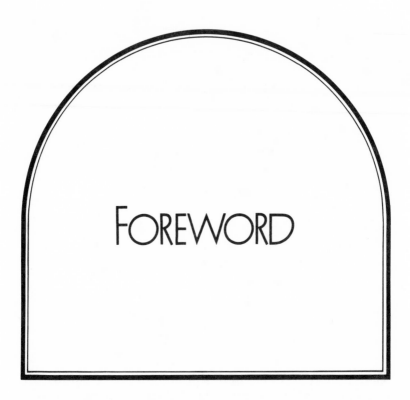

FOREWORD

With this new book Bernadette Roberts situates *The Experience of No-Self* in the broader context of the spiritual journey in the Christian tradition. Together, these two books form a major contribution to the world's treasury of mystical theology and contemplative wisdom. Ms. Roberts' experiential approach clarifies several important points that have remained obscure in the writings of Christian mystics of the past. Primary among these is her affirmation that the state of Transforming Union is a preparation for a further stage of divine transformation which, for lack of any classical Christian expression, she calls the experience of no-self. In classical Buddhist language, this stage corresponds to *dharmakaya* state of being, together with the further development, which is called *svabhavikakaya* state of being. Ms. Roberts has thus pioneered a new level of Buddhist–Christian dialogue that can lead to immense progress in mutual understanding and enrichment.

Ms. Roberts' special gift as spiritual writer is her capacity to articulate the ineffable. The clarity and sharpness of her insight and expression, her honesty about herself and her experience, the balance and groundedness of her psychological perceptiveness, and her sure touch in distinguishing accidentals from essentials—the straight and narrow path from dead-ends—make her account unique among the works of spiritual writers. Nowhere in Christian literature can one find such an abundance of detail about the state of Transforming Union nor a clearer statement of its place in the context of the whole spiritual journey.

Ms. Roberts points out the limitations of earlier writers insofar as they have overemphasized secondary aspects of the contemplative path. Their tendency to dramatize the unitive states continues to perpetuate popular misconceptions that discourage many from entering upon the contemplative path or prevent them from continuing it.

A point that may prove to be of great interest to Christians is the understanding of Jesus that Ms. Roberts' contemplative experience opened up to her. In Christian theology, the traditional understanding of Jesus formulated by the Council of Chalcedon is undergoing rethinking in terms of modern historical, psychological, and evolutionary insights. Ms. Roberts' personal spiritual experience throws a remarkable new light on the significance of the Incarnation, death, and resurrection of Jesus, both for himself and for his followers. In these two books she explores the full implications of Jesus' teaching on the nature of the transformation which his death and resurrection have made available to the human family.

Thomas Keating

THE PATH TO NO-SELF

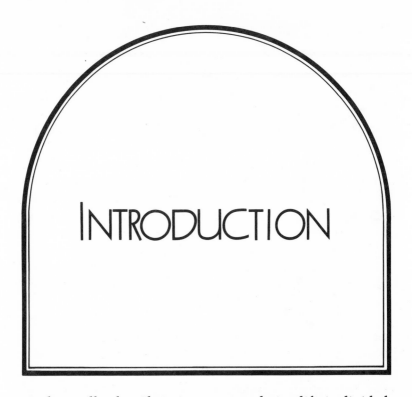

INTRODUCTION

Traditionally the Christian contemplative life is divided into three states, or stages, of progress: purgative, illuminative, and unitive, with the last regarded as the definitive, most perfect attainment of the soul in this life. While the following pages are concerned exclusively with the unitive stage, it is with an eye to viewing it as a transitional, rather than as a definitive step in the contemplative journey. The reason for this perspective is that the true end of the unitive life is to lead the soul out and beyond itself and, consequently, beyond its unitive life. Although there is no name for this step beyond union, I have described it in my book *The Experience of No-Self,** and simply refer to it as the state of no-self.

The unitive life comes to an end when we pass beyond the self and its personal wholeness to enter the

---

* *The Experience of No-Self: A Contemplative Journey* (Shambhala Publications, Inc., 1984).

3

greater Wholeness of God, wherein God is no longer known relative to the self, but instead is known as He is in Himself—known as He knows Himself. Thus, where it was once thought that only the beatific vision was wanting from our earthly union, it is now discovered that the Eye seeing Itself, or God's own vision of Himself, is compatible with earthly existence and not outside the limits stretched by the unitive life. It is only after this final going-out of self, however, that it becomes possible to look back and view the unitive state as a transitional or preparatory stage, rather than as an end, or the final spiritual stage, of man. What the final stage really is, or how far God will stretch man's original design, no one knows: all that is important is that we impose no closure or finality on the Creator and His creation.

The opening-up of a dimension beyond union neither deprecates nor supersedes the unitive state as a peak experience, or as the necessary gateway to what lies beyond. On the contrary, when viewed as a means rather than an end, we come to an understanding hitherto unknown and unrecognized of the unitive state; it opens up to man a potential that exceeds even his highest expectations of a life of union. At the same time, by raising our sights we can let go of the false aura of awesomeness that so often surrounds the notion of contemplative union, and thereby allow it to be recognized for what it is: the humble flowering of the full, mature life in which every adult is meant to live.

Once we realize experientially that God completes our humanity, we begin to live fully: that is, we courageously begin to tap into every facet of human potential, to plumb the depths of self-knowledge and to explore every aspect of our being. Only when there is no potential left to tap—nothing left to experience, nothing left to learn or discover, nothing left to suffer—only then are we ready for God to draw us beyond these personal limitations, draw us out and into the boundless secret of His existence and His potential.

What the unitive life is, then, is an active, progressive death to the self: the same self that is in partnership and oneness with God, the "true self" hidden with God in the deepest center of being. But with the final disappearance of this unitive self we come to the realization that where, at the beginning of the unitive life, complete loss-of-self could only be known in a transient experience of full union, ecstasy, or total suspension of the faculties, here, at the end of the unitive stage, loss-of-self becomes a permanent reality, a reality made possible by a life of practical, selfless giving. Thus, a final and complete loss-of-self is not achieved by ecstasy, spiritual marriage, or by any such comparable experience, but rather by years of such selfless living that, without satisfaction accruing to the self, the self must die. What makes this selfless giving possible, however, is the self's initial union with God: outside this union, this particular type of giving is not possible.

In turn, this means that the unitive state is the prime state of selfhood, of wholeness and integration, which gives rise to man's most productive years, because the energies created by this union never wane and are ever moving outward beyond the self. This is also the state in which, for some, holiness can be achieved because holiness belongs to the suffering self, a self able to give unceasingly without receiving in return—a life devoid of self-satisfaction. Once beyond the self, however, holiness is no longer possible because now, there is nothing left to give and no one left to do the giving.

It has been said that the fullness of the unitive life is a rare achievement. Yet for the man who relies on grace, the unitive life should be his ordinary expected goal, a goal realized rather quickly when the dedication is sufficient. The contemplative, in particular, comes to this

state in a short period of time, because the explicit supernatural help he receives shortcuts the same terrain others
travel over a longer period; in fact, it is this rapid movement that defines the contemplative life. But whatever
the time involved, it must be kept in mind that the unitive state is the same for all, because the mysterious nature of this oneness cuts across all spiritual diversity and
individual experiences, experiences that always and
everywhere are subordinate to union itself.

It is a great disservice to God and an underestimation
of His generosity for authors on the contemplative life to
tell us that the unitive state is the special prerogative of
saints and mystics. The exalted, often euphoric language
some authors use to define this state, fictionalizes it to
the point at which many contemplatives cannot identify
with it even though, experientially, they know the state
all too well. It is important, therefore, to take a realistic
look at the human dimensions of union and, if necessary,
strip it of the extraordinary phenomena, transient experiences, and emotional language that have nothing to do
with the state itself. To help us do this, we must adhere
as closely as possible to St. John of the Cross's oft-
repeated distinction between union experienced as a habitual, substantial state, and union experienced as a transient "act," which is accidental to the state. When this
distinction is not clearly defined, there is a tendency to
mistakenly define the unitive state in terms of what, on
close inspection, is actually a transient experience. Thus,
throughout this journey, we must keep in mind the difference between what is substantial and what is accidental,
and draw clear lines wherever necessary.

In order to focus as closely as possible on the various
aspects of the unitive life, the following chapters have
been divided according to the state's most noticeable
phases, turning points, or milestones. Because these di-
visions are based solely on personal experience, the reader
is cautioned to take what he finds with a grain of salt and

not as dogma or the discovery of a new way. The way I traveled the contemplative path is actually very old, common, and traditional, so if there is anything new in these pages it stems solely from an individual perspective. What follows, then, is a personal account, but one that has been restricted to the experiential milestones that mark the phases of unitive life.

Not a great deal has been written on the unitive state, and what we know is taken mainly from the lives of saints and mystics of such antiquity that we cannot but wonder how they would fare in the ridiculous psychological and social milieu of modern times. As representative of the mentality and religious tenor of their times, we might expect the saints to appear differently from one age to another; for even if man is not in the process of "becoming," God is always coming new to man, always keeping pace with his time and his knowledge and, in this way, revealing himself uniquely from age to age and from one individual to another. Thus, if man's union with God is not changing, his view of this union and how he lives it will be ever subject to change and variation.

In taking a new look at the unitive life, this book attempts to expand our knowledge of it, primarily by viewing union as a transitional rather than a definitive stage. At the same time, it is hoped that, by setting our sights beyond the state itself, we may come to see it in its proper place, as a state realized not only by every sincere contemplative, but as the true state in which God intended every person to live his mature years.

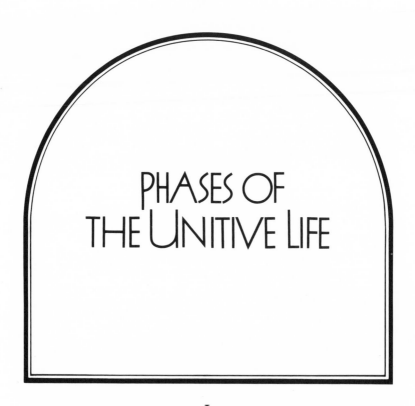

PHASES OF THE UNITIVE LIFE

I

By a conviction born of experience, I mark the definitive entrance into the Dark Night of the Spirit as the first phase of the unitive life. Here begins the cauterizing, the burning-through to the deepest center of being, which is painful and shattering to all aspects of the self. The deep, deterministic reins of self-control have been taken away and the will power that glued together this fragile unity has dissolved. From here on, the reins of our destiny are in the hands of a greater power, a higher Will, and though we may unconsciously kick against the goad in painful rebellion, it is all to no avail. The only way out is to be submissive, to accept our helplessness and to recognize that peace of soul—the day it can be found—is our greatest ally. With no place else to go, nowhere else to turn, we have no choice but to go down into the depths of our nothingness where, at rock bottom, God eventually re-

9

veals Himself and discloses to us the rootedness of our existence in Him. Thus having traveled through the bottomless void of our being, we eventually come to rest in a deep union with God—the abiding stillpoint at the center of being.

II

The second phase begins with the discovery that, where there was pain, now there is peace: from here on, the work of the soul is to maintain this peace against all movements to the contrary. This is done by remaining passive to the peaceful, still center and by submitting everything to it, for we now begin to glimpse that, at bottom, this peace is the silence and stillness of God Himself. From this point on, we have continuous access to this stillpoint of our existence to which all aspects of being must now conform, so that no movement of mind or emotion can rob us of its silence or move us from this center. One learns how to do this through the process of an active passivity that ultimately brings about the self's new form of unification. Around this center will come together all the shattered, fragmented pieces of self that had been displaced and unhinged when the center opened up. This process of re-formation is the making of the whole person—the new man—an integration not made or maintained by human hands, but by the power and magnetism of the center drawing all parts to itself, reordering them in a way hitherto unsuspected by the soul. After this, all parts will function as a unit, all acts will derive from the center, and when this unifying process is completed, the Night of the Spirit is over.

III

This third phase represents the peak of the unitive life, ushering in the fullness of the contemplative experience.

In this unified state, the continuous interior silence is much like the habitual prayer-of-quiet that, because it is habitual, appears quite natural and, of itself, constitutes the backbone of the unitive life. Apart from this, either at times of prayer or when otherwise not occupied, all the faculties enter into this silence and remain for long periods lost in God. Here too, due to the silencing of the memory, we become familiar with a certain sense of loss-of-self which is unspectacular and impermanent. From the depths of this interior union is born a great strength, an accumulation of the power and energy of love that, after drawing us inward, would now move us outward because it cannot be contained within. This love is the burning flame that would suffer every trial and forfeit its life and experiences to be able to give as it has received. The strength of this generosity will constitute the turning point of the unitive life, acting as the preparation for all that follows. It is as if we had arrived on top a mountain and asked, Where do we go from here? What is left to be realized? Until now, the movement of life had been one of interiorization and unification but, once completed, this movement turns around and, with a thrust of inexhaustible energy, moves us out beyond ourselves to a life of selfless giving. Thus arriving at the peak, we have no place to go but down, a coming-down, however, that is a going-out—a more complete going-out of self.

IV

The fourth phase of the unitive life is the active phase that follows the same path and comes to the same end as Christ's active life. In other words, it is the way to Calvary and the crucifixion, the final death of the self. This phase is marked by the continuous flow of exterior trials, tests, and every type of suffering wherein the soul finds its sole refuge hidden deep in God—deep in the center that lies below the joys and sorrows of earthly existence. Those who meet with success, renown, or any form of personal glory or satisfaction in this phase must forfeit Calvary because they will not be ready, will not have undergone the necessary preparation to come to Christ's own ending. By the very nature of the unitive state, the man of God moves contrary to the flow of this world's thinking and behaviors—so much so that his very existence in the world is antagonistic to it. And because he sees differently, he is forever destined to walk alone, totally alone. Thus, the way forward is to be rejected, misunderstood, and subjected to every conceivable tribulation—in a word, it means to live fully. In time, it is realized that the great desire to return measure for measure, to give as we have received, to do or die, has all been a subtle form of self-seeking. Where we had thought the inexhaustible flame belonged equally to God and self, we now see it was never for the self to use either for God or for neighbor, since the result would have been some form of self-expression or self-gratification. Now, we see there never was and never can be any adequate earthly form of expressing this unitive love, because from beginning to end the flame never had any other purpose than to burn us out, wear us down, and thrust us out of ourselves without any accompanying sense of personal satisfaction: in truth, this flame is not our own. But by the time we see this, selfless giving has become a habit, a way of life. We cannot live otherwise, we cannot turn back. Thus we must go forward to the final consummation: to the final death of self.

V

Although it falls within the active phase, this fifth step of the unitive life—which I call "the open mind"—is so vital and important that it justifies a separate treatment. This step leads to the finest blossoming of the unitive life, which is charity—a movement of further growth and unmasking of the self. The day comes when we realize great limitations have been created and imposed on us by our personal frames of reference, mental constructs, judgments, and patterned ways of thinking, all of which have virtually closed us in upon ourselves. To step outside our patterned constructs—which have an easy answer for everything and therefore prevent us from learning anything new—is difficult to do because it means stepping outside ourselves. This process may take years of insightful effort and practice. The final key to this going-out seems to be the cessation of judgments, which are based on how things should be rather than on how things are, and therefore shroud the reality of the here and now with wishful thinking. When these judgments come to an end, however, the mind is opened to a depth of caring and understanding wherein there is nothing reserved for the self, and until we come this far, all relationships and good works are but masked self-seeking. But to come to this point takes insight, courage, and even risk-taking, because it means leaving behind all personal securities and intellectual crutches. Yet this opening-up is urged and abetted by the unitive grace: it is part of the outward thrust in the search for what lies beyond the self—true charity, which is the ability to give selflessly without the subtle, unconscious need for self-satisfaction. In this way, the open mind is the key to going beyond the self, the key to true charity, the key to the silent mind, and the key to the very purpose of the unitive life.

VI

The final phase of the unitive life coincides with the final demise of the self. Over the years, the deepest roots of self have been subtly dying—a dying largely hidden from consciousness because the deepest self lies hidden in God, and only gradually and imperceptibly is consumed by Him. Unknowingly, we have been stripped to the bare roots of personal existence, and are now prepared, poised on all levels of being for the final emptying. Initially, for myself, this phase was marked by a disturbance at the center. The interior flame rose up to become a burning torch, a great love wherein the last vestige of self-awareness was but a flickering match. But when the flame rose up, other unknown powers and energies rose with it, which gave rise to certain extraordinary experiences—as if I were about to be used as a medium. Because this role of medium was unfamiliar, incongruous with past and personality, it was judged unacceptable, but I finally knew it was worthless because it was obviously mixed with self—a self that could no longer deceive or entice. The denial of these energies was the unwitting denial of the deepest roots of selfhood—the same self which is one with God. This denial is difficult, but once done, the energies disappear and in their place is a blessed, divine stillness. At this point, there seems to be a return to the middle of the third phase, in which the faculties are continuously absorbed in silence, but unlike the third phase, the major feature of this silence, is the imminent loss of self-awareness. Also, this silence no longer gives rise to any flame—energy or interior strength—because all is immovably still. Thus, after years of an inward, unifying movement, and more years of an outward, selfless movement, here, at the end, there is no movement at all; and here too, ends the unitive life. It seems that perfect interior silence, with the final cessation of self-awareness, is the necessary vehicle to span the gap between self and no-self, after which a new life opens up, a life that remains inconceivable until it is lived.

DICHOTOMY OF EXPERIENCE

To preface a book concerned with contemplative experiences, it may be of interest to point out that they can be divided into two major types: experiences "above the neck" and experiences "below the neck." What these terms lack in sophistication, they make up for, I think, with their accuracy.

It is often misleading to try to pinpoint the mysterious aspect of our experiences by attaching them to some known faculty—will, memory, intellect, consciousness, or other aspects of mind and feeling. While these terms may be useful in certain areas of investigation, they become inadequate when applied to the contemplative dimension, in which it is obvious that man has other, unknown faculties for communicating with God—faculties which cannot be activated on any other level of knowing or experiencing, but are perhaps reserved for God alone. In describing areas of origin and concentration, the terms "above" and "below" adequately account for the dichotomy of experiences; it is unnecessary to use more academic terms, which do not foster any more accuracy or any better understanding.

I first became aware of this dichotomy at an early age, and thereafter followed this phenomenon throughout my contemplative life. Over the years I made numerous discoveries, but none as relevant or as clarifying as those I made after the falling-away of the self. What I discovered is that the self—or that which may justly be defined as self—is made up of two distinct experiences: one is the experience of self-consciousness made possible by the reflexive mechanism of the mind; the other is a gut-level feeling of personal energy or power. I believe these two aspects of the self constitute the core of all personal experience, and correspond accurately to the dichotomy of contemplative experience as well—types I refer to as "above" and "below." The drama of the interior life centers largely on these two aspects of the self, because these are the aspects that will undergo alteration, change, and transformation, and act as mediums through which grace is experienced—as long as self remains. Thus, as we move through the contemplative life, it is interesting to notice how these particular aspects are continually being affected either separately or together, and how, in the end, they will be totally silenced, stilled—put to their eternal rest.

Examples of experiences "below the neck" are the sense of presence, infusion of love, prayer-of-quiet, will-to-God, and living flame of love. Here, too, we encounter the true center of being, the stillpoint, and realize our union with God, along with varying levels and degrees of interior silence. From the center arises the peculiar pain of God's absence, the wound of love, and the peace which surpasses understanding. There are other delicate movements in this region, but, altogether, these experiences are responsible for a sense of deep interiority and spirituality, and because of these experiences we say God is "personal."

Although feelings of sentiment and emotionality also arise "below the neck," I exclude these as authentic receptors of the supernatural; in every case, they denote spiritual immaturity and give evidence of a grasping self. Not only are the emotions the antithesis of pure spirit but, if clung to and not relinquished, they will abort the contemplative journey altogether. Supernatural infusions we call "love," "peace," and "joy" do not arise from the emotions, but bypass them as inadequate receptors of grace. If the emotions try to enter into an experience, they will only dissipate it, because they try to drag down to a lower plane that which can be received only on a higher plane. The nature of grace is to lift us out and above these lower levels of being, and since emotionality, by its very nature, is self-centered and not God-centered, it has no place in the unitive life. But then, St. John of the Cross brings this out quite clearly in Book II of *Dark Night of the Soul*, as well as in numerous passages in the *Spiritual Canticle.* *

In the following pages, the terms "love," "joy," and "peace" must not be understood in their usual emotional context. It is unfortunate that we do not have a language specific to the contemplative experience, because using equivalent terms to describe two different levels of experience invariably leads to erroneous interpretations. This happens not only with emotional terminology, but worse, in the conceptual area as well. The description of a non-conceptual way of knowing, of experiencing reality and truth, is a hazardous employment that never sits well with the dogmatic, academic, or even ascetic mentality. But what are the choices? Either the contemplative takes

---

* Saint John of The Cross, *Collected Works*, translated by Kieran Kavanaugh and Otilio Rodriguez (Garden City, N.Y. Doubleday, 1964).

his risks and speaks out, or remains silent for fear of being misunderstood. History tells us that contemplatives have always accepted the challenge, and have become outspoken witnesses of God's ways with man. If this were not the case, the deepest, most divine dimension of human experience would remain locked within—an enclosure which is contrary to the contemplative movement itself.

Experiences I call "above the neck" have to do with consciousness and the mental faculties. This would include certain forms of enlightenment, one of which is the impression of a sudden light in the mind, whereby some truth of God is revealed or invisibly "seen." The mind is also the seat of the contemplative gaze—the silent fixed look upon the Unknown—which I believe is due to the suspension of the reflexive mechanism of the mind. Since the intellect has numerous functions, or movements, any one of these, or all of them together, can be suspended, held in silence, or plunged into a darkness which can be painful or peaceful. Here we encounter the cloud of unknowing, self-forgetfulness, and the true origin of ecstasy. Once the doors have been closed on our ordinary way-of-knowing, we come upon a nonconceptual way-of-knowing that, because it is not filtered through any known faculty, is virtually impossible to account for. This way-of-knowing has no true counterpart in concepts, ideas, images, or even in our vocabulary.

The coming-together of these two types of experience—above and below—gives rise to a more wholistic form of experience—the prayer-of-union, or various degrees of union and ecstasy, ranging in intensity. It seems that the nature of the wholistic experience is to take us out and beyond our self, beyond all sense of personal interiority, in order to impress upon us the All, the Everywhere, and the unity of God. But whether above, below, or in combination, the most noteworthy aspect of these experiences is the ultimate silencing of the self, because this is the way that leads to pure experience, which is nonrelative, or outside the self.

Although the experiences I have listed are few in number, the fact that they are well known to most contemplatives suggests that the great variety of descriptions we encounter may be due to the various receptive states within a single individual, rather than to the variety of individuals involved. Take, for example, the same grace given to an individual in three different stages of his development. As a beginner, the contemplative may feel himself seized and overpowered by a great force; as a proficient, he may only notice a subtle change or alteration in his ordinary state; later yet, he may realize this same grace as his habitual, quite natural state of being. In between, of course, we may expect a variety of responses, impressions, and descriptions. This does not mean, necessarily, that God's grace is the same for all—or even for one—but it does suggest a commonality of experiences that cuts through sheer numbers and lays stress instead on the various receptive states of the individual. At the same time, this implies that the most common bond, or shared grace, between contemplatives is the silencing of the individual self, and that this silencing defines the most basic character of the contemplative movement.

Apart from this silencing, other types of religious experience, no matter how lofty, mystical, or supernatural, would not, in my opinion, define the true contemplative. I have always held that St. Teresa was a mystic who had a few contemplative experiences, and that St. John of the Cross was a contemplative who had a few mystical experiences, because the difference between these two saints is so great that, without a shared doctrinal basis, their paths might never have crossed. Though any experience of grace may be called "mystical," the mystics of history were largely noted for the phenomenal character of their experiences, i.e., visions, voices, etc., which are not common among ordinary contemplatives. It is the shared grace of silence that tells us we are all headed in the same direction and that, being drawn by the same force, we will ultimately come to rest in the same end—the same God.

In retrospect, it would seem that the predominant experiences in the unitive stage are centered "below the neck," because it is this aspect of self which is most in need of immediate transformation, unification, and silencing; without this, we cannot move to the next step, the step beyond union. This next step occurs when we come to the point where there is no longer any movement within, or "below," and the emphasis shifts to a radical change of consciousness* and a consequent shift in the region of experience from "below" to "above." When this change is complete, however, there still remains a certain dichotomy of experience, for even without a "within," the diffusion of love (God) becomes like air without boundaries, while, at the same time, the Eye seeing Itself is the overriding habitual state. I regard the Eye seeing Itself as the greatest of great realities, but one that has its beginnings early in the contemplative life as the fixed gaze upon the Unknown. This gaze is not only the meaning of the word "contemplative," but the essence of its experience and, in the end, the contemplative's habitual state.

There is at least one experience I know that does not fit into the duality of experiences I have been discussing. This experience is the simple, matter-of-fact seeing of God as transcendent—that is, God outside, beyond creation, "impersonal," and therefore nonexperiential. This is a kind of nonexperience because it neither touches nor affects us in any way, but is as simple as a cloud passing

---

* The phrase "change of consciousness" is not found in older, traditional texts; nevertheless, it is the psychological reality of the dark night of the spirit, or first major change of consciousness.

by, about which nothing more can be said. This type of experience is puzzling because it seems to have nothing to do with the interior life, and does not tie in with our other experiences. For myself, I took it as God's way of reminding me not to get bogged down or caught up in my personal little world of experiences because, in the long run, He was beyond them all. At the same time, I knew that, on my own, I could not reach the transcendent: only the indwelling Spirit could bridge this gap, and, if the transcendent and I were destined to meet, it could only be through this Medium.

Little did I realize that one day these transcendent experiences would become the whole of it. With the falling-away of the self—and consequently the falling-away of the personal indwelling Spirit—all that remained was the transcendent God, God beyond all personal experience. It was then possible to look back and see how these simple experiences had been a clue, a preparation, and an intuition of what lay ahead.

It would appear that God has three paths of communicating with man, paths that correspond to the three aspects of Himself as Trinity. First, the indwelling Spirit, our true center, seems to be God's most obvious, universal manifestation to man, or man's most immediate experience of God. Second, but less obvious and not as often experienced, is the unmanifest aspect of God as first cause, transcendent to creation, the seeing of which would have nothing to do with a personal self. The third is by far the most difficult manifestation of God to get hold of. This is the experience of Christ, who is too subjective to be objectified, for in Christ we realize the saying: God is closer to us than we are to ourselves. As Christ is the very life of the soul, how can we get an objective look unless we stand outside ourselves as objective observers? Thus, Christ is our most subjective experience of God. We are not transformed into the Spirit; rather, it is the Spirit who transforms us into Christ, and while the Spirit continues to remain objective to us, Christ does not—in truth, he cannot.

The true nature, then, of our nondual experience of Christ lies in our identity with Christ, for whom the Spirit remains as object of consciousness. Thus, in the unitive state, we are one with Father and Spirit, but identical with Christ in a type of dual/nondual realization of the Trinity. It is only later, when all self-consciousness—Christ-consciousness—falls away, that God-as-object gives way to God-as-subject, or when the Oneness of the Godhead is realized beyond the Trinitarian God known to human consciousness. It is this transition from God to Godhead that I have tried to describe in *The Experience of No-Self.*

Nothing, perhaps, so attests to the subjectivity of Christ in ourselves as does the Eucharist, the bread of life which must be consumed to be fully realized. Here, Christ is flesh of our flesh and soul of our soul. Meister Eckhart went so far as to say that "We are totally transformed into God as in the Sacrament the bread is changed into the body of Christ"*—thus comparing our identity with Christ to transubstantiation. Christ is not in his proper place in our lives as an object of veneration; rather, he is the subjective one in us who recognizes and obeys the indwelling Spirit, knows Him as an object of love, and ultimately lifts us up and out of our self to know the transcendent Father. There is nothing about a man's self that can do any of this. The self can do nothing: it is utterly helpless in this matter.

As I see it, when Christ said he must go to his Father in order to come to us, he meant that as long as he remained exterior, as an object to be seen, he could not be fully realized within us, and, therefore, his mission re-

---

* Raymond Blakney, *Meister Eckhart: A Modern Translation* (New York: Harper and Row, 1941).

mained incomplete. To complete his mission, Christ must subjectively transform and perfect humanity through the invisible work of grace from within, and impart to man his vision of Spirit and Father. Thus, Christ is the most subjective and mystical of all contemplative experiences; gradually, imperceptibly, he replaces the subjective self until, in the end, without a self, he is all that remains.

A final note on the dichotomy of experience has to do with the notion of God as personal or impersonal. As long as self remains, this dichotomy persists, because the nature of self-consciousness is a subject-object, dualistic way of knowing and experiencing, and matters will remain this way until we go beyond the self to encounter a totally nondualistic type of knowing. When this dichotomy falls away, God is realized as pure subjectivity, closer than close, the Eye seeing Itself without reflection, a type of "seeing" indescribable and inconceivable. Nevertheless, God turns out to be more intimate and "personal" than even the relative term implies—although not personal relative to "you" or "I," or relative to any "thing" at all. What this means is that, beyond self, God-as-impersonal has no ultimate validity or truth; whereas God-as-personal takes on a whole new meaning and experience. Thus, God is personal in that He is all that exists—all, that is, but the self.

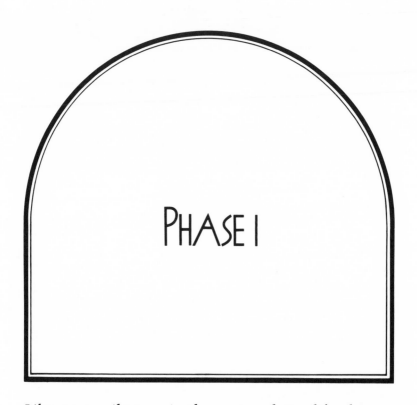

PHASE I

Like every milestone in the contemplative life, the entrance into the Dark Night of the Spirit is heralded by a definitive stroke of the supernatural, which means that, in a single moment, we are cut off from all that went before, and placed in a new dimension, with no possibility of going back. Where nature's acts are groping and vacillating, supernatural acts appear decisive and irreversible. It is this particular character of the milestone that makes the contemplative life a continuous, forward movement, for, even if we go no further, neither can we go backward. Thus, a stroke of the supernatural appears to be a permanent, irreversible alteration of nature itself. From this point on, all we can do is acclimate to a new dimension, state, or, simply, to the inevitable.

Because of the irreversible character of such a milestone, I have often pondered the endless warnings of contemplative writers against backsliding, infidelities, sin, and all the rest—as if one could merit this forward thrust, or, thereafter, alter it in any way. If, say, a man without a parachute is suddenly hurled from a plane, he is given no choice as to the path he must take. Even if he abandons his will to God the fact remains: he has no say; his destiny is no longer in his control. He can panic, curse his fate, or cling to a passing bird, but he cannot alter a thing, he cannot go against the flow. Such, at least, is how I view the contemplative milestone, and define the experiential reality of a supernatural act.

The milestones that mark the contemplative path are well-known to me and, on occasion, were as benign as if the man hurled into space suddenly discovered he could walk on air; yet, for the most part, these acts struck me with the terrible seriousness and mercilessness of an almighty God. Although, now and then, a divine sense of humor relieves the continuous tension between God and soul, the frightening truth is that God is not playing games with man: He is in dead earnest, and He intends to hold man to his true destiny, come what may.

These milestones, or forward thrusts, seem to be a stretching of man's nature, a continuous stretching for an expanded knowledge of God—what He is and how He works. Every act of God is a creative act: it is His revelation and manifestation, the very essence of what He is; therefore, a supernatural act is God's business, a business that He takes most seriously, because this is His life! But what of the man in the plane who has been so rudely shoved from his position of security? Surely he is the victim of an irrational and unmerciful act? Since only the Creator knows the true nature and destiny of His creature, only He knows the way forward, for, in this respect, man does not know himself, and therefore does not know his proper direction. Thus, the man falling through space is in good hands. Though he does not know it, in the end he will not so much as stub his toe.

For myself, the entrance into the Night of the Spirit

26

was just such a merciless milestone, a thrust beyond personal security. It happened as follows: I had been reading in the garden when I felt an invisible film, or thin veil, come down over my head, and shroud my mind. Instantly, I knew something had happened, but no idea came to mind, nor was there any other response. Swiftly and decisively, all had been done in silence; yet, however simple and innocent its quiet descent, this act was, in effect, terrible and awful—the Almighty had simply lowered the boom.

The first thing I noticed was that I could no longer see the words on the page; suddenly, they had become characters without meaning. It was several days before I could read again, and then it was totally without meaning. For years afterward, I could only derive meaning when and where God permitted some understanding to break through; these breakthroughs would shed light on the mystery of God's ways in my soul, in creation, or in his great plan for man. Because the contemplative state is always changing, this special light is also changing, always either leading the way or keeping pace, I do not know which. Apart from the practical knowledge necessary for daily living (horse sense), my mind was plunged into darkness, wherein the only way of knowing was by this special light; I had to trust it implicitly, because there was no other way of seeing.

An example of how this light works occurred in this initial stage of the night when, through dim eyes, I could suddenly identify with the anguish expressed in the Psalms, which now seemed a perfect echo of my state of soul. Years later, however, I no longer found any personal meaning in the Psalms because, by then, the state had changed. Thus, no insight or enlightenment lasts forever; rather, it comes and goes, shedding light on our present state, ever assuaging the human need to know. In this way, what strikes us as inspiring at one time will, at another, leave us quite empty—which tells us we must cling to nothing, because all is a passing gift, and not the end of the light.

Although the mind is now left in a painful, empty void, this symptom is actually the lesser of two that mark this phase of the dark night. If it is dark and empty "above" (in the mind), so, too, it is dark and empty "below" (in our interior). After the descent of the veil, I looked inward to encounter not the usual, obscure presence of God, but a gaping black hole where He had been, and on seeing this, there arose from this center a pain so terrible, so enormous, that I wondered how it could be contained. It was the feeling of being cauterized, branded by God in the depths of my being—depths I never knew I had till then. The pain was beyond control, verging on the limits of human endurance with no escape or cooperation possible; in a word, the pain was all!

For the next nine months, this pain came and went as it pleased, in daily bouts, several times a day. My understanding was that God had some merciless work to do here, and would not relent until His mysterious job was done. In time, I toughened enough to be able to take the pain with a modicum of stillness—without buckling interiorly, that is—and was therefore able to watch this burning-out process more objectively. I discovered that the nature of the pain, at this point at least, was an unconscious (unintelligible), unwilled rebellion, but a rebellion I found puzzling. Since, on the surface, or conscious, level, I was willing to bear the pain, how was it still possible to have this deep inner rebellion? It has been said that a house divided against itself will fall, and this, I believe, is what happened. With the eventual disappearance of this pain, there was never again any such disunity of will, or disparity between the wee, small voice that helplessly affirms: I will endure; and that deep, fighting spirit that says: I cannot endure! I have noticed that, despite its apparent "surfaceness" and total helplessness, the wee, small voice is always right—it always wins out.

Eventually, I learned that the best protection against this pain was to fully accept it, and that by virtually sinking into it, sinking into my feeling of utter misery and nothingness, the pain lost much of its punch. It seems that a deep submissiveness is essential here, because, with the increasing ability to hold still, let go, sink in, and thereby come to naught, the pain subsides, and eventually disappears. After this came peace of soul, and, though it was initially loveless and joyless, it was, nevertheless, as painless and restful as the calm after a great storm. Then, from out of this nothingness, this ash-heap of misery, there gradually emerged a whole new life.

As it happened, I went through the dark night alone and at an early age, with no previous knowledge or instruction regarding either the contemplative life or its various stages. Yet, for this reason, I had the advantage of coming through with no preconceived expectations, theories, or ideas regarding the true nature of the night, or what was really going on here. Having gone through previous states of grueling aridity, I took the night in much the same vein: as a test of endurance, a trial of love, a period of toughening up. Later, when reading St. John of the Cross's description of this night, and recognizing myself well enough, I was nevertheless struck by his theoretical framework or explanation, which I found curious, even questionable, because I was convinced that such an explanation could not possibly be proved by the experience itself. Thus, for example, I had no impression of this passive night being a process of purification, unification, or transformation, or that its darkness was caused by an excess of illumination. None of this was given in the experience itself; rather, this is what is seen in retrospect. It is a post-experiential theory that attempts to make sense of the experience. There is nothing the matter with doing this, of course, because every theory expresses man's search for a rationale for his experiences.

A problem arises when, accepting a theory or conceptual framework as ultimate truth or proven fact, we plug our experiences into it, and thereby let go of our initial impressions—impressions that are the sole validity of the theory in the first place. We do this because somehow the theory says it better, explains it all, and lends a value and importance to our experience that otherwise might not be there at all. When a theory raises an experience out of its mundane reality, we are on a mind-trip; that is, we are placing a conceptual value on a nonconceptual experience. Because I had a tendency to do this myself, it was necessary to continually throw out all theories and explanations as possible overestimations, if not inaccurate statements, of what I felt had happened—or was happening.

The reason for bringing this up is twofold. First, I believe the value and validity of contemplative experience rests solely on the experience itself—never on any theory into which it can be plugged. Nothing is to be gained, and a great deal is lost, when we fit our experiences into an acceptable framework and think no more about them. We will never expand our knowledge of the contemplative life this way; we may even bog down in an illusion and, possibly, go no further with our interior Guide. Second, there is a notion afoot that every contemplative must somehow make his experiences conform to a particular theoretical framework—as if mere intellectual acceptance of a theory could do that. This process leads to nothing more than an acceptable form of dishonesty. The threat, of course, is that if you do not see your experiences in a particular light, then you do not belong to the tradition at all. St. John of the Cross was once called a Buddhist by an individual attempting to throw the saint out of his own tradition because he could not be reconciled with this individual's idea of how things should be.

30

This is what happens when there is rigid adherence to a theory, personal insights, or points of view—as if anyone had the final word on these matters. What is important is that we leave the door open, not only to the views of others, but to the infinite possibilities of God and His ways of guiding, enlightening and bringing man to his final destiny.

There is no question that the Dark Night of the Spirit is an authentic stage in the contemplative life; it is a powerful movement and one that will turn us around for the rest of our lives. But on a theological and psychological level, we do not know the exact mechanism of the night; we do not understand the supernatural reality of what is taking place, nor can we fathom the subtle, imperceptible workings of grace. Indeed, this very unknowing typifies the state. What we do know, however, is what our experiences tell us—our honest impressions, sufferings, insights, the changes we notice, the general course of things, and so on. This is all we really know.

What follows is my impression of the night, and though quite positive about what I learned, I know it is not what others have learned; I would be the last to say: this is what everyone should learn. What I have to say is not definitive; it is not a theory. It is only the attempt to give a different view of the night and, by doing so, hopefully to expand our knowledge of it.

With the appearance of the black hole and the ensuing pain, I had the impression of being burned to the depths of my being. At times, this hole seemed to be only the pit of my own misery and nothingness, a bottomless pit that went nowhere. But at other times, I looked into the depths of this hole to see God eye to eye, and, realizing this as the most marvelous of sights, I took courage and opted for more pain—as if that were possible.

One day, at the end of this initial phase of the night, I reached bottom and knew I had reached it, knew there was no going down any further. At bottom—the deepest level of being—all was dark, still, and peaceful; I felt it to be a level far below the emotions, thoughts, and their combined movements. From here, all life's activities appeared relatively superficial, inconsequential. Shortly afterward, I discovered that at this level—pain's end, so to speak—my existence, or all I knew of it, came to an end, and God's existence began.

Life at the bottom is much like the description of the prayer-of-quiet, which is said to be a state of interior silence in which the will is one with God. At bottom, I made continuous contact with the silent stillpoint of existence, which then became a continuous awareness, an awareness, I believe, that underlies and characterizes the unitive life. It was when God revealed Himself as the stillpoint that I discovered my true existential union with Him, for at this point the divine runs into the human and imparts true life to the soul. This finding was accompanied by a great certitude, one which formed the backbone of my unitive life and all that followed. I might add that this certitude was experiential, not derived from intellectual belief. When the painful knowledge of human contingency is burned into us, it gives rise to a different type of faith, one that, because it is experiential and nonconceptual, no longer depends upon intellectual knowledge.

The discovery of this deep, existential union was not the discovery of a new union formed between God and the soul, but, rather, the discovery of a union already existing—from the beginning, or from the moment of creation, perhaps—a union that had been there all the time in the depths of being, but was only now fully revealed. Traditionally, the discovery of a pre-existing union is not regarded as the highest find in the contemplative life. Instead, it is held that the highest form of union is a union-in-the-making where, at one point, God is said to marry the soul to Himself in a special, experiential, supernatural way. For the mystics, of course, this marriage is accompanied by visions, and the exchange of rings and things.

But looking deeper, I ask: Is our deepest union with God made at a single point in time—a moment of vision, perhaps—or does this union already exist, and is it simply revealed to the soul at one point in time? To ask it another way: Is the contemplative journey a process of becoming one with God, or is it the process of stripping away the superficial layers of self in order to realize, in all its great reality, a union that has always been there?

Before turning to St. John of the Cross for a possible answer, I must state, for myself at least, there was never any experience that suddenly informed me, "Now you are one with God." In fact, when this union was first revealed, I realized I had known the state, or had been in it, for some time, but was only now seeing it for all it was worth. What this recognition brought about, however, was a change in awareness; what, until then, had been obscure, now blossomed into full consciousness—a passive consciousness—which could then be used, but how the consciousness of union is used is understood at a later phase.

However it comes to us, the realization of our union with God is always a grace, a kind of mini-milestone. Without this particular recognition I, for one, might have lived fifty years wondering if I was ever going to come upon the unitive state. These revelations, or graces-of-recognition, are essential to the unitive life. Unless God reveals our union with Him, we have no way of identifying the state, no way of understanding the reality of what we experience in the depths of our being. Indeed, unless God identifies Himself, we have no way of knowing Him at all. As a child, I had numerous experiences in which God did not identify Himself *as God* until years later. I do not know why he does not always reveal Himself as God, but instead, remains an unidentified power within. My guess is that he only identifies Himself as God when it is necessary to match up to a person's conceptual beliefs. Thus, I spent my early childhood looking for two things: God, and the true identity of the mysterious power within, because the two never matched up in my mind. Only when the mysterious power identified itself as God did the two come together. Even then, I was skeptical, because it was too good to be true; it was beyond belief. In some ways, all our experiences of God are beyond belief, because all conceptual beliefs pale when compared to the experiential reality.

In the dark night, God can no longer be recognized in the way He was before; at bottom, He must reveal himself all over again. Now He will be known in a new way, far more subjective, wherein He is hardly objectifiable anymore. The journey inward and downward has shattered all previous ways of knowing God and self; it has burned into us the painful knowledge of contingency, dependency, and the recognition that, without God, we are nothing—capable of no good. Having come to the end of our personal resources, we meet God at the existential crossroads, and realize that in our ending is also our beginning—the beginning of a new life of union, which will become the source of contemplative peace, joy, love, and freedom. Compared to the depths of this union, all other experiences in the unitive life will ultimately appear superficial. What it takes to make our oneness with God an experiential reality is what the dark night is all about: it is the painful revelation of our deepest union with God, one that existed from the beginning, but only now is revealed in its true, existential depths.

To examine more closely the nature of contemplative union, I turn now to St. John of the Cross, whose description of the unitive experience is without equal. As preface to what follows, I first acknowledge my indebtedness to the saint, who was the only human source of illumination during my contemplative journey. If I should appear critical anywhere, it must be understood as an in-family difference, not as a negative reflection on the immeasurable value of his works, or on the truth of what he describes.

When speaking of the true nature of the soul's essential union with God, St. John of the Cross is not always clear or consistent; at times, he is even confusing. Earlier, we referred to his distinction between a habitual union made in the substance of the soul, and a transient union, or "act," in which the faculties are more or less suspended. But there is another distinction he makes when he speaks of the essential union between everything created and its Maker, a union he refers to as "natural." With this latter distinction, we now have three types of union, or three ways in which God is united to the soul. Confusion arises when, in the course of his works, the saint uses the same terms—"essential" and "substantial"—to refer to both a natural and a supernatural mode of union. This is brought out in the following passage, where he calls attention to these three types of union.

Here I only intend to discuss this total and permanent union in the substance and faculties of the soul. And I shall be speaking of the obscure habit of union, for we will explain later, with God's help, how a permanent actual union of the faculties in this life is impossible; such a union can only be transient.

To understand the nature of this union, one should first know that God sustains every soul and dwells in it substantially, even though it may be that of the greatest sinner in the world. This union between God and creatures always exists. By it He conserves their being so that if the union should end they would immediately be annihilated and cease to exist.

Consequently, in discussing union with God, we are not discussing the substantial union which is always existing, but the union and transformation of the soul in God. This union is not always existing, but we find it only where there is likeness of love. We will call it "the union of likeness," and the former "the essential or substantial union." The union of likeness is supernatural, the other natural. The supernatural union exists when God's will and the soul's are in conformity, so that nothing in the one is repugnant to the other.

—Ascent of Mount Carmel, *Book 11, Ch. 5*
Collected Works.

From this passage, it may seem that we are being asked to dismiss once and for all the consideration of our natural union with God, since this is not what the saint intends to discuss or describe. But to dismiss this natural union is not only impossible; the saint does not, in effect, do this himself. He will continue·to refer to our deepest, supernatural union as "substantial" and "essential," because he is being true to the unitive experience itself, though not so true, perhaps, to a conceptual, theological interpretation.

It would be impossible to cite the numerous places where the saint has reference to our first existential union with God, but in the passage "Reveal thy presence" (*Spiritual Canticle*, Stanza XI), where he speaks of the three modes of God's presence in the soul—which correspond to the three modes of union—he does not seem to care whether God reveals Himself naturally or supernaturally, just so long as He reveals Himself. What is obvious, however, is that the God to be revealed is the same God with whom we have our natural union, the same God whose natural presence we wish to be revealed. *What is supernatural, then, is not the presence or the union, but the revelation itself.* It is pure grace.

A passage which has significant bearing on the true nature of contemplative union reminds us that, just as everything created has a natural center, so, too, the natural center of the soul is God.

36

The deepest center of an object we take to signify the farthest point attainable by that object's being and power and force of operation and movement ... When once it [the object] arrives and has no longer any power or inclination toward further movement, we declare that it is in its deepest center.

The soul's center is God. When it has reached God with all the capacity of its being and the strength of its operation and inclination, it will have attained to its final and deepest center in God, it will know, love and enjoy God with all its might.

—The Living Flame of Love, *Stanza 1,*
Collected Works.

Further on he adds:

And thus, when the soul says that the flame wounds it in its deepest center, it means that it wounds it in the farthest point attained by its own substance and virtue and power.

—Living Flame, *Stanza 1,*
trans. Peers.*

Sometimes we forget that man, as he was originally created, has his center in God. It is part and parcel of his being; without this he could not exist. But man displaced this center by putting his self there instead—virtually trying to make himself God—and thereby obscuring God as his natural center. But when, by grace, the self is displaced—as happens in the dark night—man once more recognizes God as his true center, a recognition that is not conceptual or a matter of mere belief, but one that comes

---

* *Complete Works,* translated by E. Allison Peers (Westminster, Md.: Newman Press, 1964).

through experiential contact. Because grace is the means by which we return to our original, unitive center, we think of this union as supernatural. But, in truth, the means is not the end. Our end is the same as our beginning—our original union with God—which is, in turn, the same union realized by the contemplative in the unitive state.

As the self is displaced and God is disclosed, we marvel at the transformation and regard our union with God as truly spectacular, which it is. But as we acclimate to this new life—life as it was originally intended to be—this state of union feels like the most natural thing in the world: a union that is beautiful but common, wonderful but unspectacular in its daily living. In the excitement of the return trip, we lose perspective on many things; we may think we have left everyone and everything behind—including ourselves. But, in reality, we are just beginning to live as we should: to live a life in unison with God.

By postulating two unions, natural and supernatural, certain misconceptions arise regarding the true nature of contemplative union. The fallacious aspect of this dichotomy is that if everything is traced back to its original source, everything but evil ends up in God—nature and grace included. The only way I can see any truth in this dichotomy is in the recognition that a world of difference lies between a conceptual belief in our existential oneness with God as a "natural," logical deduction, and the experiential or "supernatural" realization of this oneness, which is contemplative union. The difference, of course, is as great as between the unreal and the real.

St. John of the Cross does not get into the dispute concerning what is natural and what is supernatural, but instead affirms that man has one deepest center of being, a center in which he discovers his union with God, and thereby taps into the fountainhead of love, the same love that created him in the beginning and sustains him in the present. For the contemplative—that intrepid explorer of being and witness to God's ways—to realize any type of union of a lesser, more superficial nature is inconceivable. Some authors, however, would have us believe that the ultimate contemplative union is some type of affective, or emotional union of love, an idea which is patently false, and nowhere to be found in St. John of the Cross. The saint tells us time and again that union cannot be grounded in, or properly experienced by, the emotions; such a lower faculty is incapable of entering into union, and any overflow experienced is a sign of weakness, a soul not perfectly purified or conformed.

The few references the saint makes to an "affective love" should be understood in the Thomistic sense of rational psychology, where the term "affective" refers to the will, not to the emotions, or "passions"—as the saint calls them. There is a link, of course, between will and emotions; in fact, the will stands in a unique position as mediator between mind and emotions. Yet the emotions belong always and forever to the self, while the will has the capacity of belonging equally to God and the self, as a kind of shared faculty. The union of wills abandons the self's feelings of its own love, in order to enter into God's own love—love beyond all emotionality.

I can find no place in St. John of the Cross where he affirms that God and the soul are in a process of becoming one, or that union is in the making; rather, he affirms that the whole of the contemplative movement is the process of realizing our oneness with God on ever-deepening levels. As he says, man has numerous centers and unions, all of which must be passed through and left behind in order to reach the deepest, centermost union, which is the same union, but realized at its deepest level.

From my first reading of the saint, I interpreted his continual references to "an essential union made in the substance of the soul," as an experiential contact with an *already existing union*, a union made by God alone, not by the soul and God together. My reason for this was that, from early childhood, I had numerous unitive experiences of God, and found in the saint's writing an explanation for the continuum of my experiences that, otherwise, could not be accounted for if union were viewed as something achieved at a particular point in time, or at some peak of the contemplative life.

What changes in life, then, is not our union with God, but the modes of its experience, its levels of realization. Thus, man is in a process of awakening to ever deeper and more perfect ways of realizing his oneness with God, a oneness which remains stable and immutable from the beginning, and remains so to the end.

My concern here is simply to clarify the true nature of contemplative union. I certainly have no axe to grind; I was not deprived of the graces and experiences to which St. John of the Cross alludes. If anything, I have known a surfeit. It was in suffering a surfeit that I discovered a saturation point in our experiences, beyond which the only remaining desire is for the absolute, final truth of God as He is in Himself—that is, God unadulterated by any concept or experience into which the self could get a toe or a finger. At this point, I realized the truest thing I knew, the greatest truth ever encountered, was the deep, abiding, existential oneness with God, which is of more worth than all experiences put together, because it is the only truth that goes beyond the self and refuses to be polluted by the self. There is no doubt about it: this center is the way out.

Referring to our unitive center, St. John of the Cross calls it a "point" beyond which the soul cannot go, where no further movement is possible. This center is the silent stillpoint of existence around which all interior and exterior movements revolve; it is an immovable center that becomes a fortress of peace and strength for us.* But how,

---

* For another interesting view of the "point," see *Living Flame of Love*, Stanza 2, verse 10, *Collected Works*.

we may ask, do we know this stillpoint is truly God? Unless (at this point) God reveals Himself, we have no way of knowing, because only God can confirm this identity, and give us the certitude needed to move us to the next phase of the dark night—the coming-together of the whole man around this center. Thus, to proceed, we need God to identify Himself. Then we can have absolute trust in this center, abandon ourselves to it, become passive to it, and have no fear; otherwise God cannot accomplish this unifying work in us.

As we can see, merely to discover the center of being is not enough. God must let us know that this is His kingdom, where we have union with Him, and where, from now on, we must learn to dwell with Him. We need grace to come to this point, grace to realize the center for what it is. Finally, we need grace to learn how to live and act from this unitive center.

To represent the nature of the soul's union with God, St. John of the Cross makes use of numerous analogies, many of which are applicable to the experience of union as a pre-existing reality, but a reality disclosed at one point in time. One of these follows:

A ray of sunlight shining upon a smudgy window is unable to illumine that window completely and transform it into its own light. It could do this if the window were cleaned and polished. The extent of illumination is not dependent upon the ray of sunlight but upon the window. If the window is totally clean and pure, the sunlight will so transform and illumine it that to all appearances the window will be identical with the ray of sunlight and shine just as the sun's ray. Although obviously the nature of the window is distinct from that of the sun's ray (even if the two seem identical), we can assert that the window is the ray or light of the sun by participation.

The soul upon which the divine light of God's

being is ever shining, or better, in which it is always dwelling by nature, *is like this window, as we have affirmed.*

—*Ascent, Book II, Ch. V, (emphasis mine).*

From the beginning, God's light has been shining on the soul, but the soul could not comprehend it until all obstacles to vision had been removed. Though we may not always be basking in this clear light, the certitude of what is seen is ours forever, and, with this certitude, we go forward. There is far more to the unitive life than the recognition of our deepest union with God, but this recognition is where it all begins.

The above analogy is pertinent to what we have been saying, not only because it illustrates the work of the dark night and verifies union from the beginning, but because it raises the question of how this union is seen in retrospect, when the window becomes so clean we can no longer distinguish the window from the light shining through it. When looking through a window at a very real, clear view, we wonder if we are looking through a pane of glass or not. One way to find out is by touch, by feeling the window; another way is by having seen the window in a previous or different light—perhaps when it was dirty. So too, there comes a time in the unitive life when we can only distinguish our identity from God's identity (in this center) by having had previous knowledge of the window, having seen it when it was dirty, which is a kind of knowledge in retrospect. This knowledge is important because, apart from the sense of touch, or the "feeling" of a separate identity, we can no longer "see" a separate identity; we can no longer see if the window exists, because the light is so bright. From here on, when looking deep into the center of being, we no longer see a self but see God instead—and here comes the temptation to say that our true self is God, when, in truth, our true self is a self united to God, and hidden with Him in the deepest center of being.

The proof of this is that, despite seeing only God at the center, we nevertheless retain the feeling of selfhood, or "I am," because the eye looking inward—that which is aware of the unitive center—is the subjective, witnessing pole of self-consciousness. Union is not the eclipse of both poles of consciousness; if this were the case, there would be no knowledge or experience of union, no knowledge of self and other. Union is the bond of two powers at the center of being—or the center of consciousness, the objective pole of consciousness, whatever we wish to call it. Thus, although we no longer see self at the center, we still retain a feeling, or sense, of personal selfhood.

But, to take this a bit further, let us say that one day we went to the window and discovered we could no longer even feel it, no longer feel the self as a separate existence—what could be said of this? Evidently, someone has removed the window and, when we went to feel it, we simply fell out, literally fell out of our self. The possibility of such a happening is the intriguing aspect of this particular analogy; if we cannot see or feel the self anymore, what becomes of a separate identity? As it stands, however, this particular problem does not arise in the unitive life: here, we continue to feel our separateness, even though we may not be able to look within and see any distinction in the center.

So far we have been considering the nature of union, and how its discovery is made possible by the wound inflicted in the dark night. Now we must move on to take a closer look at the particular aspect of our being that touches upon God, and forms the mysterious link between the human and the Divine.

Earlier, we were told that a "union of likenesses" was a conformity of our will with the will of God; since the soul's union (which is this conformity) takes place in the deepest center of being, we can conclude that the deepest center of being is the will. But if by "will" we mean the faculty of desire, choice, or other volitional movements, then we are not going deep enough, for union with God on this level would only create a robot. One of the unique characteristics of the unitive life is complete freedom of will, which opens up all of life's options to us, and explains the statement: love God and do what you will. What we need to look for is a deeper hold on God which makes this complete freedom possible.

It has been said that, consciously or unconsciously, man seeks the highest good, and that he cannot help seeking it, because it exerts a pull on him that never gives up. Those who go against this force, naturally, do not seek and do not find, but those who follow this path of least resistance will automatically be pulled to the center of their being. I call this magnetic pull a "will-to-God" which, at the same time, is possibly as much as we can "feel" of our union with God on an everyday level. In the unitive life, it is raised to a level of continuous, passive awareness.

Prior to the dark night, our desire for God was merely our consent to this inward pull; it was our active effort, will, or desire to find God as our minds had conceived Him. But, during the night, this active effort is replaced by an active passivity, because God, who draws us along, is the only one who knows the right direction. This direction is not conceived by the mind, not even known to the mind and, therefore, cannot be followed by the mind. In a word, the depths of the descent, and the passivity required, literally boggle the mind—go beyond anything we thought possible. What enters into union with God is not our mind, but our will-to-God, which is that particular aspect of self fashioned by God solely for Himself, and which, in the dark night, has finally come home to rest.

I regard this passive will as a separate faculty of soul, not to be confused with the ordinary active will or faculty of desire. This will-to-God has been passive to God from its beginning; it has always faced Him. But the active will, which is totally self-oriented, exerts itself to keep us on the surface of life, chained to a limited mentality. The active will must be incapacitated, made immovable, before the passive will can rise to the forefront of experience, and consciously be recognized for what it is—that aspect of self which belongs to God alone. Once this is accomplished, the active will again takes up its ordinary life, but this time it takes its proper place as subordinate, and conformed to the unitive will-to-God.

When deep calls upon deep, what do we hear? What is conveyed in the union of wills? Since God's first will is that we exist, it follows that our first will is also to exist, to exist for God, which means being what we were created to be. So, on the one side of our unitive center we are totally passive to God, and, on the other side, completely free to be what we are—totally human. Thus, it turns out that our will-to-God is equally our will-to-be. We can now accept ourselves and our human lives without fear of going contrary to God, because now there is no contradiction of wills. To realize the fullness of human freedom, then, and to exercise it without fear, there must be total acceptance of our self and our present lives—such as they are. This may sound easy to do, but, in truth, it is extraordinarily difficult.

Somewhere in the back of the contemplative mind is the creeping illusion that union with God means to be a little more divine than human, a little more extraordinary than we actually are. We keep waiting for this to happen, and cannot understand why the union realized in the depths of our being does not come forth to the outside, or why it does not possess us completely, take over our humanity—make us completely divine. This search for perfection—which is a search for divinity—is nothing more than the failure to accept our existence the way it is.

As I see it, a problem arises when the search for a satisfying self-image is based on conceptual notions of what perfection is, instead of on "what is"—our everyday reality. Man's notions of perfection are invariably relative, speculative, and superficial; unconsciously, they are subtly self-centered. Since only God knows what He has created, knows its true perfection, all we can know or experience of this perfection is what we learn in silence, where will runs into Will. Letting ourselves be guided by this passivity at the center is difficult, because it means going contrary to our intellectual theories and expectations of perfection; going contrary to our self-image and how we think we should be; and, more often than not, going contrary to society and those around us. To be perfectly passive—to belong perfectly to God—is the most difficult of human accomplishments. But we cannot even begin this difficult journey until we first discover our abiding union with Him; for, without this, we cannot let go of the self by accepting what we are, nor can we become passive to the center by entrusting it with our final destiny.

In ending this discussion of contemplative union, I call attention to the fact that God does not communicate His will to us on a conceptual basis. If he did, His deepest union with man would be mental—a kind of union of intellects. But the center of our union is on a deeper level than mind or intellect. It is in the very center of existence, which I call the will-to-God. This will is a silent faculty; it does not think, speak, remember, or form images. It is a silent power that takes its power from God, and in this silence our will runs into His will, there to receive its life, strength—virtue. To know the will of God, we have only to remain silent, remain in the still center which, automatically, without a single thought, is the perfect acceptance of the present moment, and what we are at the moment. Thus, all the intellectual searching, including the often agonizing efforts to ascertain the will of God, is nothing more than the refusal to accept the present moment, and our present state. The secret of the unitive life is the graced ability to live in this passive silence of wills, a silence which is always here and now, and always one with God. The truest communication with God is absolute, total silence; there is not a single word in existence that can convey this communication.

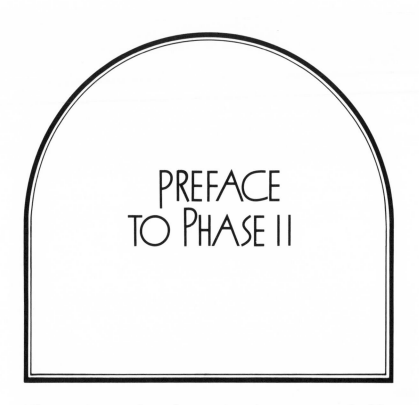

PREFACE TO PHASE II

The opening up of our deepest interior center may be likened to an underground explosion, wherein all parts of being are sent flying out of control and scattered in every direction. Prior to this experience, and by virtue of a strong will, we had fashioned our own unity according to what we knew of its parts, and thereafter held these parts together with the tight reins of self-control. In a word, we were masters of our own house. The entrance into the dark night, however, shatters this man-made unity. From here on, God takes over the reins of control and becomes master of the house. From His central position, He gathers together, as a magnet draws filings, all fragmented pieces of psyche and soul, reordering and refashioning them according to His original design. Thereafter, He holds our being in unity by the magnetic power of His will, His presence—His love.

The first phase of the dark night is the painful revelation of our deepest union with God; the second phase is the unification of the self around this center of union. Thus, the unification of the self automatically follows the soul's realization of its existential union with God, and when this second unity is completed, there will emerge the new man—the integrated, whole, God-centered man. Once this dual unifying process is accomplished, the work of the dark night is over.

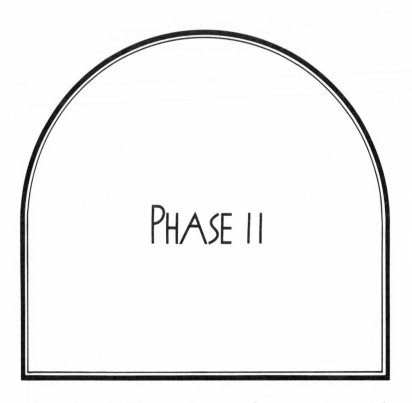

PHASE II

Where there had been pain, now there was peace, and though initially dark and dry, it was deep and restful. After nine months with no peace of soul, this gift was seen as a merciful lull, which I expected to dissipate any minute, but when it did not happen, I understood the pain had spent itself, done its work, and would not reappear. Though later in life, certain trials would bring me again to the threshold of this particular pain, the peace at the center never gave way; it held firm as a gratuitous, defensive wall which nothing could penetrate. It was as if, upon touching this wall, all hurt, anxiety, and suffering would dissipate, dissolve, and come to nothing. In this way, suffering became a joy because it was a reminder of God's faithfulness, and the enduring strength of our union.

I soon discovered this new state of peace was more than the absence of suffering: it was the gateway to God which had a way of spreading joy like the infusion of a subtle air, an air which could be described variously as joy, love, or the "peace that surpasseth understanding." Enamored of this peace, I sought it day and night, and thereby discovered it to be the key to the unifying process. I discovered that the foundation of this peace, or its underlying reality, was a deep interior silence and stillness, and that the infusion of love acted as a lure, drawing the soul down into the depths of silence.

Initially, this peace was found only in the deepest center; outside, the mind and emotions were roaming about, unable to enter this deeper dimension, and they were therefore at a loss for an object to which they could become attached. Their continual movements were disquieting and distracting: they drew attention away from the center. Thus, it was obvious that all was not perfect; the house was still divided against itself. Periodically, however, all such movements would come to an end, and in the subtle power of total silence—above and below— there was a foretaste of a state to come. These foretastes of full union were like a light in the passageway, allowing me to see ahead and take my direction—a direction which was to have implicit trust in the silent center; for here, trust was the only way forward.

The key to the present movement is to remain passive to interior silence, to trust it as we trust God Himself, and to let nothing take us from it. While this center acts as a magnet drawing everything into itself, in order to be wholly drawn in, we must first abandon all that is contrary to silence—all the disturbing movements of mind and emotions. We gradually abandon these by remaining passive to the center on the one side, and passive to the movements on the other—that is, we let the movements pass, not getting mentally involved; because as soon as we do, we move out of the silence and into the fray. By remaining passive, however, we learn the knack of being objective about our thoughts and feelings, and come to see them for what they are—superficial, without depth, perishable, fickle, disturbers of peace, and totally incompatible with life-at-the-center. As long as we can objectively observe our thoughts and feelings, division remains, but when there is perfect unity, this observing is no longer possible.

In time, the center of silence is discovered to be a place of refuge from disquieting movements, an observation point, a kind of defensive fortress which these movements cannot enter—they can draw us out, but they cannot enter in. By habituating to this fortress of peace, we are unknowingly putting aside old ways, habits of acting and reacting—the buildup of years—in order to learn a new way of life, which is life-at-the-center. Thus, the center becomes the point of reference for all movements outside itself, and the gauge of all life's responses. I might add that, once we acclimate to living and acting from the center, our life becomes filtered through it in such a way that we become incapable of seeing anything apart from God, because he colors everything, everywhere we look.

When we come to the point where these movements no longer disturb the inner peace or draw us from its silence, these movements grow weak, fade, and eventually come to nothing—they no longer have power over us. Thus, the center gradually frees us from the tyranny of the lower faculties; once we are no longer slaves to mind or emotion, we have come upon the essence of human freedom. By remaining passive to the center, it has become everything to us: not only the center of being, but the center of all interior movements that now have reference to the center and are subject to it.

The unique aspect of the unifying process is that it does not come about through our own effort or self-control—through anything we do. At this stage, all our interior activities and strivings are but disguised efforts to regain the reins of personal control and return to our former ways of behaving. Our part is to remain passive to the inner silence and trust it. This trust is so imperative at this time that I would say the speed with which unification is completed is proportionate to the degree of passivity. The passivity required is at the level of our deepest wellspring of being, our will-to-God, which is the root of selfhood and personal existence. Since this will is a power that takes its power from God, it must be passive to God in order to be perfect. Then, too, as mediator between mind and emotion, the will, now rooted in God, effects a balance between these lower faculties, a balance not maintained by our own efforts, but maintained automatically, unconsciously, by the will's passivity to God—our center.

Before the dark night, we had united our will to God by our own ascetic efforts, but this union was impermanent, superficial, and, being dependent upon our self, without eternal stability. Now, however, we must release our hold on God, because it is He who will hold us in unity, and hold us at a level where our own efforts count for nothing—a level we cannot reach through our self. In releasing our hold, we may think we are letting go of God when, in reality, we are only letting go of our self—our grasping strangle-hold on the satisfaction we derive from our own efforts, our own doing, our own strength of will. This letting-go is not easy; it demands a great trust, which will extract the last farthing of self-abandonment. We need not fear we are giving up God, or even our self; all we are giving up is our limited way of knowing and experiencing God and self. To come upon a superior way of knowing, we must first give up what is inferior.

In some ways this process can be compared to the action of a centrifuge, wherein all parts assume their rightful place and are held there by the dynamic energy at the center. The result is the whole person—stabilized, balanced, working as a unit, with all parts going in the same direction. Thus, God holds everything together in unity, and, as His marvelous and original design, the soul must indeed be beautiful for Him to behold.

Again, it is as if we had come upon an interior treasure so great that everything outside holds no value for us; we desire nothing because we already possess everything. We are utterly content within ourselves and need nothing outside ourselves—the inner treasure is sufficient unto itself. No experience in life has the depths of this center; it is a depth that belongs to God alone; it is His domain that remains untouchable to all outside. At this level, only God can touch or affect us. When living at this level becomes a habit of soul—when nothing can draw us out—then there is no division remaining; all is conformed to the inner silence, the entire house is quiet, and the unifying process is over. We are now ready to move on.

To summarize this far: once the deepest center of being opens to us, its silence becomes increasingly accessible as a refuge of peace. We are subtly lured into this center by infusions of joy and love which increase our desire to remain in this dimension. In itself, this dimension is both a conscious awareness and a subtle feeling of deep interior space, a space so deep it seems at times to go through our being and out—beyond ourself. As we acclimate to living in the center we lose the old habit of being swayed by thought and feeling because they can no longer draw us out, disturb our peace, or reach to this deeper dimension. Thus, the process of learning to live at the center is the process of unification and transformation, otherwise known in contemplative literature as "transforming union." It means we are losing old ways of acting and responding in order to learn how to live at the center in union with God.

When all aspects of self are in silence, but before reaching the full unitive state, we may come upon a mysterious plateau of silence, a plateau that may be the cause of some concern. Once we have been lured into silence by the infusion of joy and love, all such infusions come to an end, and we are left in silence, wherein there seems to be no God, no self—nothing but silence itself. After abandoning all to God, we seem abandoned by God, and although there is no anxiety or pain, there is the temptation to move out of this silence, which means moving back into our old frustrations. Right here we seem to have come to a dead end; we are trapped because we cannot go backward and do not see the way forward. This is a crucial point in the unitive movement. But it becomes a problem only if we make it one, which we can do from sheer ignorance. I know, because I did. Nevertheless, we are standing at the gateway to the very peak of the unitive life.

As stated earlier, the infusion of love and joy were lures drawing us into an underlying silence but, once we enter this silence, we must be weaned from these lures and become acclimated to a totally silent state, for God is deeper than His gifts, and what we want is the truth of God Himself. So we must not cling to or become dependent upon even those experiences we valued before; soon they will be seen as relatively superficial compared to the deeper dimension we are about to realize.

This plateau is actually our time of becoming rooted in silence, rooted until this silence becomes the deepest, most stable habit of soul, the deepest aspect of our existence. This plateau is the test of passivity, abandonment, and trust, and it may be a helpful deterrent to look back on the pain and frustration we encountered when moving out of this silence. We have been too burnt to move, learned too well the lesson: of ourselves we can do nothing. The only choice is to remain patient, silent, and to be resigned to this state as long as God wills.

Once ensconced in complete silence, it would appear the unifying process is over, but, in fact, there is still something wanting; mere silence and continuous peace are not enough. It is from this plateau of silence that we are taken to the peak, which will be the revelation of God in some fashion, and I can think of no other rationale for this revelation than that we have become sufficiently acclimated to a silent state. Before this time, such a revelation would only have reinstigated the disquieting movements of the lower faculties—thoughts, emotions, and other responses that stand in the way of a continuous awareness of our abiding union with God. Thus, when the revelation comes, we will be ready to take it in stride—in silence—because now we are perfectly prepared to do so.

It was at this point or plateau of silence that I came upon a particular problem. Although it is not in the books, it will be worth mentioning because this problem may be well known to many contemplatives and, if nothing else, will illustrate the type of fears that can arise during this particular phase of the journey.

At this time in my contemplative life, I was eighteen and in a convent. A novice mistress had just been appointed who was new to the office and new to me. One day, she asked about my prayer, so I told her: I do nothing; there is just silence. This astounded and upset her; without asking another question, she told me in so many words: because my prayer was not in keeping with my virtue—I had none—it was obvious I had gone wrong somewhere, and was probably suffering from illusions such as St. Teresa described in those who think they are more advanced than they are. My prayer was nothing more than a "natural" silence, and therefore not from God; it was a form of quietism—a heresy in the Church. She ended by saying the devil could well have his hand in this; he was leading me to think I must remain silent, when all the time I should be practicing mental prayer.

This came as a great surprise because I had never heard such things before; never heard the word "quietism," never heard that there could be illusions in the life of prayer, and had no idea why she thought I was trying to put myself up as an advanced soul. But most shocking of all was the notion that I was being led by the devil!

My immediate impression was that she had got me

all wrong, and because there was no attempt to understand, she obviously did not want to understand and, possibly, was incapable of doing so. I decided then and there never to speak to her again of my interior life—and I never did.

For her part, however, she did not give up so easily, and for years she assiduously kept after me, pointing out every lack of virtue and each imperfection. All this, I was convinced, amounted to nothing more than personality differences. It was obvious I did not fit her mold of perfection and could not be made over into her image and likeness. There is no use going into the petty details of such a problem; let it suffice to say that it was a great problem for me.

She managed to scatter in my mind the seeds of doubt and fear, fears of all sorts, fears that wanted to draw me from silence into disquiet and anxiety. Though I recognized the source of these fears, this was no help; they persisted for a long time, until God mercifully wiped them out one day in a single definitive sweep.

But the worst part of this trial was being caught between God and my superior, each wanting me to go in a different direction. There was no question of being active in prayer; I had learned the painful way that this was out of the question. But I had the fear that, instead of standing firm in the interior silence of God, I was only standing in the silence of my own self-righteousness—a kind of stubborn stance that said: I am right and she is wrong. It seems I had to defend my peace of soul by putting up a wall between myself and my superior. This is a terrible position for a religious soul.

Later I discovered this problem was well known to St. John of the Cross. It motivated, in *The Living Flame of Love*, his classic tirade against spiritual directors who insist—out of ignorance—that their clients be active in prayer at a time when God requires interior silence and passivity. But then, this tirade was delivered four hundred years ago, which goes to show there is nothing new under the sun; contemplatives through the ages meet with the same problems.

At any rate, this trial may have accelerated the unifying process by forcing me to dive to the bottom in search of silence. It taught me, as nothing else could have, what a mighty fortress of peace, what a bastion of strength the center really is. While living in the center does not make the external circumstances of life any easier, at least it makes them possible—meaning, we do not run away, but stay to take what comes with peace and equanimity of soul. This is much like suffering without suffering. It is not pleasant to walk through fire, but the marvel is that we can do it at all—without being burnt.

Another invaluable lesson was the imperative to always follow God's interior direction, and to be wary of all direction coming from the outside. Since the nature of the contemplative movement is the intimate revelation of God's mysterious ways in the soul, it is totally a One-to-one situation. As someone pointed out, it means being alone or "al–one," as the word implies. Even those who have traveled a similar path cannot get into our soul any more than they can get under our skin; they cannot do what only God can do. There is no such thing as three-way direction. It is always inspiring, of course, to discuss our interior life with others, to get their opinions and views, but as for their leading us anywhere, it won't work. When it works, the soul bogs down in human attachment and dependency that work against it; sooner or later, all such "help" must be given up.

Remaining passive at this stage is crucial; we may not understand this, because it seems to go contrary to our former habits, contrary to the way we think we should go, and contrary to the way others tell us to go. The notion of passivity, as far as I know, has never had a high rating with contemplative authors. The word is anathema to the ascetic athlete, for whom it means doing nothing, backsliding, or falling from grace. It takes a tougher soul to remain passive through thick or thin, because it means going contrary to the self and the gratification the self derives from its own doing. The ascetic, on the other hand, hangs onto the self for dear life, thinking he is hanging onto God. Unknowingly, of course, he has mistaken himself for God, so that what he (the self) does, has the stamp of God or "God's will," and what God does, has the stamp of nothing. Until he sees his mistake, he cannot enter the contemplative camp.

St. Therese of the Child Jesus took much of the negative sting out of the notion of contemplative passivity by calling it the "little way" of abandonment and trust in God. This means the acceptance of our littleness and helplessness when we come upon the vision of great disparity, or come to naught in the night. Though some identify the "little way" with other levels of the spiritual life, I think it had its beginning in this stage of the unitive life. Right here, the only way forward is by passive abandonment, when we allow God to carry us—as a parent carries a child—across an otherwise impassable terrain. Apart from this passivity, there is no other way across—simple as that.

Because in the contemplative life we often encounter trials that are due to sheer ignorance, we wish God would shortcut these trials by telling us outright what we are to do, which way we are to go. Though this solution sounds simple, it would turn out to be virtually worthless. God's verbal instructions would be miles away from His experiential movements within the soul, movements that inform (as they transform) in a totally nonconceptual way. To think that God speaks, communicates, knows, or has an intellect that is akin to man's, is simply to make God into our own image and likeness. There can be no communication comparable to grace, which is the movement of true life Itself. To say to a tree, "Grow!" is meaningless, but to get inside and cause the tree to grow is comparable to the workings of grace.

We can sit for years watching a tree grow without witnessing a single movement—though the tree might have grown six feet. Like grace, its growth is silent and imperceptible. This is how God brings about a maturity and perfection that cannot be seen for the looking, cannot be heard for the listening and, often, cannot be understood for the experiencing. With the use of time-lapse film, we can see the tree grow, and thereby marvel at the beauty and miracle of this process. So, too, the growth of the soul can be seen only in retrospect, or when we get distance from the changes that are imperceptible on a daily level. Growth, then, is not and cannot be directed by words, concepts, or anything from without. We may think, talk, listen, and watch, but all the time God works in absolute silence, for it is in silence He lives, moves, and has His being. This is the reality that cannot be conveyed in words, but this is the reality we come upon in complete silence.

Toward the end of this stage, when beginning to see the light at the end of the tunnel, I was finally given to read St. John of the Cross. It did not take long to find this part of the night aptly described in the *Spiritual Canticle*, which book, to my knowledge, is the only one in contemplative literature that deals exclusively with the unitive life. Though the saint tells us that the book covers the whole of the contemplative journey, the opening stanza, "Wither has thou hidden thyself," is not indicative of the beginner, who usually has just come upon a great find, not a great loss. Stanzas 1 through 12 are the plaintive search for a beloved absence, the straits of a soul in dire emptiness, darkness, and affliction, which is clearly the predicament of the dark night.

In my own experience, the two passive nights were back to back, with no delightful or ecstatic interlude between—as some authors would have it. As for an intervening "illuminative stage," for myself at least, it would have to be dispersed throughout the passive nights and the entire unitive state. Had I been the one to map the original contemplative path, I would never have thought of including an illuminative stage because, from beginning to end, the interior life is an ongoing illumination; as a discrete stage, I do not find it authentic or necessary. Authors who take St. Teresa as their guide are more apt to see this stage—the fifth mansion—intervening between the passive nights. However, such a stage cannot be found in St. John of the Cross. As it happened, St. Teresa never shed any light on my interior life, but then, she was a mystic and I, a common contemplative. As I see it, one never knows where the mystic is going to be the next day; their path—if they have one—is difficult to pin down and certainly impossible to follow.

Although the first part of the Night of the Spirit is given a more realistic treatment in *The Dark Night*, I find this second phase of the unifying process more adequately described in *The Spiritual Canticle*. No other place in the saint's works contains a description of this process in such detail and with such great fidelity to the experience itself.

Stanza 13 is the report of a transient experience—a rapture, or foretaste of a state to come—which ushers in the second phase of the dark night.* The soul no longer speaks "of its former pain and yearning," because this has now been replaced by a deep sense of "peace and tranquility."

This spiritual sleep which the soul has in the bosom of its Beloved comprises enjoyment of all the calm and rest and quiet of the peaceful night, and it receives God together with this, a dark and profound Divine intelli-

---

* The saint calls this turning point "spiritual espousals."

gence, and for this reason the Bride says that her Beloved is to her the tranquil night.

—Spiritual Canticle, *Stanza 15.*
Complete Works, *trans. Peers.*

Despite interior peace, however, all is not perfect. This peace has been given only to the spiritual, most interior part of the soul, but not to the exterior or sensory faculties which, by reason of their inferior nature, are incapable of entering into the depth of the unitive experience. Thus, while we are enjoying inner peace, the sensory faculties are running rampant, playing havoc with the outskirts of the inner sanctum, disrupting the peace, and breaking up the unitive tranquility. Until these exterior faculties—fantasy, imagination, and the feelings they evoke—are silenced or brought into conformity, our union with God cannot become a continuous realization, nor can the unification of all faculties be completed.

The saint tells us the soul still has some "bad habits" left, and that all its energies of mind and emotion have not been brought into subjection. Thus the soul suffers "perturbations and disturbances coming from her lower parts," so that the sensual motions are stirred up to distract the tranquil life at the center. These disturbances he calls "foxes," which are the "chorus of desires and motions of the senses." Here they spring up to take control, "excite the imagination"—in a word, "make war" on the peaceful interior kingdom. "Even to this point comes the lust which as S. Paul says the flesh has against the spirit for . . . that which is wholly carnal finds weariness and distaste when it tastes of the spirit."

In time, the soul learns that the best way to handle these involuntary uprisings is "to quickly become recollected in the deep hiding place of its inmost being," which it discovers to be a fortress, a refuge which nothing can enter save God. This unitive center is a position of strength from which we can objectively watch the foxes of fantasy without going out to them through a movement of desire. This calm observing is not easy to do, but once we can watch with total objectivity, we begin to taste the grace of victory—when the foxes grow weak, come less often, and finally disappear altogether.

The battle between spirit and flesh, or higher and lower faculties, is the concern of Stanzas 16 through 21. Here the saint uses other symbols for the disturbers of interior peace—"nymphs," "birds of swift wing," "lions, harts and leaping does," all of which refer to the excessive movements of mind and emotions. "Mountains and valleys" are the two extremes to which these excesses tend, and the "banks" (which are not level) are the first movements in either direction. When the faculties "exceed what is just," exceed the operation which pertains to themselves, the soul loses balance; mind and feeling swamp one another, thereby making us "slaves in our own house."

By "water, breezes, heats and terrors" is understood the four passions of grief, hope, joy, and fear, the excesses of which must not only be avoided, but stopped short in their first movements. "When they [the passions] pass from being first motions into the reason, they are crossing the threshold" and disturb the inner peace, but, as long as they remain first motions, they only "knock at the door" of the inner sanctum. While this knocking does not take away peace of soul, it is nevertheless a distracting nuisance we pray to be rid of. Thus, the soul asks that all such disturbances "no longer appear on the hill," no longer "touch the threshold," the "wall," or unitive center.

According to the saint, the reason for these disturbances is the weakness of the lower faculties, which run rampant because they cannot enter into union with God. As a result, the soul asks that the "depth of this hiding place of spiritual union be of such that sense may not succeed either in speaking of it or in feeling it," that is, that the soul not be touched by mind or emotion, since these cannot respond properly to interior union. We pray they be quiet, keep their place, or better still—do not move at all.

St. John of the Cross believes another cause for these disturbances is the devil, who cannot stand losing a soul to God. Admittedly, it is difficult to understand why, at this particular stage, after having come so far, we should encounter these disturbances, which we thought had been left behind long ago. Because I have never encountered a devil, I would offer instead, that one reason for these disturbances is the fact that these lower movements had not really been put to rest at the outset, or at the time of conversion, when we threw everything out of our lives but God. What this stage seems to illustrate is that, as beginners, we had unconsciously kept these lower instincts under tight control, kept them at a distance, or did not know we had them at all. But, in the night, when this control has to be released and handed over to God, the lower instincts, which have gone unrecognized or have only been suppressed by asceticism, rise up because they have never been dealt with in the first place. When tapping into the wellsprings of being, we are also tapping into man's deepest instincts, which surprise and disquiet us. Running away with God does not mean we can run away from any aspects of our humanity. Rather, it means we can now afford, with His help, to turn and face them squarely, to deal with them once and for all—as we now do in this second phase of the night. We deal with these foxes, nymphs, and lions by remaining in our center of silence and becoming objective about their movements, seeing them for what they are, and taking them in stride with no disquieting result. In time, these movements lose their power over us, and disappear as mysteriously as they came.

But, whatever the final cause of these disturbances,

the most immediate lesson they teach is the urgent and imperative need for total unity of being, total unity with God. It is not enough to be united with God in the most interior part, we must also be united with Him in all parts. God must somehow satisfy the whole man, not just the interior man. He must show us he loves the whole of our humanity, not just the center of our soul; His love must engulf us completely and satisfy every level of existence. But can He do this?

When I came to this point, I doubted very much that God could stoop to this too human level; instead, I had expected to be elevated to His level. But what happens is a little of both—God comes down and the soul goes up—up and away, in fact. What I discovered is that God not only can satisfy the whole man, but exceeds all boundaries in doing so. He can possess us so fully as to obliterate the self, take over its existence—its very breath—and completely dumbfound us. There is left no doubt that God loves the whole of man and that our need for this wholistic love is all in the nature of things—the way we were made—and that it is God's pleasure to prove this love to man.

Were it not for the particular need of the whole self to be one with God, I would never have understood the mystic's reference to God as Spouse or Bridegroom. It is obvious that the marital symbol had its origin in this stage, and that the nuptial idea was born in the satisfaction of all parts. When the full unitive state is reached, however, there is no longer a dichotomy between higher and lower because the lower forces never again exceed their mean; they have been conformed to the unitive center, and with no crying need for greater unity, the notion of God as Spouse is no longer apropos.

In Stanza 21, the transforming process is coming to an end. The soul has become habituated or acclimated to living in its deepest hiding place, where it remains

*forgetful as one that is born away from all things, even
so the delight of this union absorbs the soul in itself
and refreshes it in such a way as to give it a charm
against all the troubles and disturbances caused by
things aforementioned.*

We have now entered the garden of delights which is enclosed by a "fence of peace," guarded by a "wall of
strength" (virtue), and in this garden the soul sleeps securely because now "it is in her power to enjoy this sleep
of love every time and whensoever she desires."

From this it is evident we are ready for—or have already entered into—the fullness of the unitive state. Because it is a gradual acclimating process, we may not be
able to discern at what point full union has become a
permanent reality. It might take a particular trial to make
us realize we can no longer be drawn out, or interiorly
disturbed, because it is by such trials the state has been
gauged all along. But however it comes, the full recognition of this state is imperative to bring about a final
change in awareness. Until this point is reached, we are
not fully aware of what is in the making; we stumble
along from one trial to another, increasingly taking refuge
in the center, and growing more adept at doing so. The
foretastes we have of full union do not tell us the state is
imminent and will remain on a permanent basis; for all
we know this might be years away. Consequently it is
always a surprise when, at some point, it is revealed that
we have come to this state, and it is now ours simply for
the "sinking in." This recognition is an obvious grace; it
is like the sudden blossoming of a flower when the fog
lifts and the sun breaks through. Equally important is the
fact that it is accompanied by a change in awareness, a
change that had been in the making, but only now becomes central to the unitive state.

To trace the change of consciousness that takes place

during the night, we must go back to the beginning experience, when the cloud first descended, because this is when the change is initiated. To some extent, we may look upon the dark night as, fundamentally, a period of acclimating to this initial change of consciousness.

As stated already, the immediate effect is the inability to find meaning, insight, or inspiration through the use of the mind. It is difficult to say why this is so; I am not familiar with the functions of the brain and cannot pinpoint what actually closes down in the area of knowing. All I know is that it is a drastic alteration in the usual way of knowing; an alteration, however, that does not interfere with the practical function of common sense—which means, for all "outside" purposes, nothing has really changed.

Some authors tell us what happens is that we can no longer use images or the imagination, can no longer meditate or make use of our former techniques in prayer, but, in truth, this is the least of it. Although I could never in my life make use of images or get the imagination on the move, I understand that doing away with these functions occurs in the first passive night, or night-of-the-senses, and therefore would not be indicative of the second night-of-the-spirit, where the alteration is far more drastic. Regarding the cause and effect of this night, St. John of the Cross tells us that God's light darkens the natural faculties of soul in order that these faculties may be supernaturally illumined. This light, he says,

puts the sensory and spiritual appetites to sleep, deadens them, and deprives them of the ability to find pleasure in anything. It binds the imagination and impedes it from doing any good discursive work. It makes the memory cease, the intellect become dark and unable to understand anything, and hence it causes the will also to become arid and constrained, and all the faculties empty and useless. And over all this hangs a dense and

*burdensome cloud which afflicts the soul and keeps it
withdrawn from God. As a result it [the soul] asserts
that in darkness it walked securely.*

—Dark Night, *Book II, Ch. 16.*

The last sentence is amazing; it testifies that the soul
recognizes this as God's work and thereby takes faith—
endures. Then, too, there is security in knowing we cannot break through the cloud of our unknowing. But if we
do not know the physiological reaction to divine light, we
are well acquainted with the mental restriction it causes,
a restriction that eases up as we gradually acclimate to a
new way of knowing and living.

At this point I discovered my mind could no longer
find a focal point within or without. Everywhere I looked
it was dark, dry, and uninteresting; nothing was able to
hold my attention. I had even been cut off from the imageless seeing of God within; there was nothing to see
anymore but a black hole.

I often wondered if the alteration of consciousness
was responsible for the appearance of the black hole or
disappearance of God. Although the self is a dualistic
mechanism—self-consciousness above, an existential
feeling below or within—in a number of experiences the
alteration of consciousness preceded an interior change.
This suggests that consciousness may be responsible for
our interior feeling states as well as the center itself. At
least I know the inner eye was struck blind before the pain
arose from the center. From here on it was both too difficult and too painful to look within; I had to look without,
to concentrate on ordinary duties and chores. This type
of concentration means giving the mind totally to the
task at hand—cooking, cleaning, or whatever—without
any interior reservations. This demands complete self-
forgetfulness and, for the most part, proved to be a great
help; at times it turned into a subtle but delightful inte-

rior state. Pulling weeds was better than prayer; indeed, pulling weeds became prayer.

This restrictive condition of mind was physically very painful. For nearly three years I was rarely without this pain—located low on the forehead between the eyes—which I always described as a "pressure behind the eyes." By placing my fingers on either side of the upper bridge of the nose, there was such sensitivity that any pressure applied resulted in an unusual sensation—like sinking into a cool, dark silence. This was like concentrating on nothingness and it brought great relief.

Never having encountered this phenomenon before, I took it as part of the merciless work God had to do, as if it were all in the course of things. I associated the pressure with an enforced silence of mind, an absorption in darkness and nothingness which absorbed the attention without providing an object of attention. Since all attempts to break through the cloud were futile, I gradually acclimated to this state and eventually came upon the contemplative gaze, which is the silent dark gaze at the Unknown and Unseen. Without question or hesitation, I know that this gaze is the greatest of my contemplative experiences; I rate it as the highest, most blessed of God's gifts to the soul. Here the pain miraculously dissolves into a tremendous stillness of mind that opens onto the vision of God, a vision without medium—it was as good as an ecstasy, and a true foretaste of a state to come.

Once interior pain gives way to profound peace and stillness, the emphasis in the second phase of the night shifts to the mind and the particular circumstances we are describing. Since all is quiet within, our problems can now be traced to the mind, for without an object—even an imageless object—to focus on, the mind is at a loss to know what to do with itself. This is why it is continually roaming about and may seem reminiscent of a ticker tape machine, endlessly running on and on, thinking of nothing, unable to settle upon anything interesting. It is this restless state of mind that plays havoc with interior peace, disturbing, distracting, and drawing us out from the silent center. I say the drama of the unitive life is primarily interior or focused on experiences "below the neck" because, apart from the contemplative gaze, the mind is of absolutely no benefit in the unification and transformation process. Sooner or later the mind will have to conform to the interior state of silence and, when it does, we come upon the full state of union.

When we come to a point where the mind is finally left in a peaceful silence—which is then its habitual state—several changes become noticeable. First, there is a continuous conscious awareness of the center (God), which seems to be a most natural and automatic function of consciousness. In fact, it may be akin to body-awareness; it is just as habitual. This type of consciousness needs no effort or active maintenance; it is part and parcel of our being. Second, when looking within, God at the center is a seeable, though obscure, presence and not, as before the night, a *felt* type of presence. Putting these two changes together, it is obvious that the mind never again needs to go in search of God.

I might add that, for myself, the second change was not too unusual. From an early age I always saw God within—even before I knew it was God. Now, however, this seeing took on depth and dimension, and was accompanied by the new knowledge that the center was no longer God alone, but also my union with God.

Having come upon God at an early age, I never came upon any center of being I could call my own, or call my "self." For me, the dark night was not a de-centering process where God was substituted for self as the center of being. Nor was the night the shattering or unmasking of a false self. In truth, I never came upon a central self at all. What I called "myself" was the totality of being wherein God was the center. Thus, if "I" was anything at all, I was everything but God—which was easy enough to account for.

As it stood, then, the revelation of an abiding union with God in the center was, at the same time, the revelation of my "true self." I saw it all at once, thus, I never came upon anything I could call a "true self" until I realized my permanent oneness with God. The reason this revelation came as a surprise was that I had the unconscious expectation that transforming union would include the whole of my being—the personality, mind, and everything that generally goes by the name of "myself." Now, however, I saw that these superficial and non-eternal aspects of being are incapable of entering into immediate union with God, and that only the deepest center—the power center of will to Will—was truly transformed into God. Nevertheless, the superficial aspects of being that form a run-on with the center will conform to the deeper aspects of union and being.

What occurs in the dark night, then, is a shattering of self and the disappearance of God, but only as these were known up to this point in time. In retrospect, we realize that it was a shattering of the superficial aspects of being in which we unknowingly had put too much faith. The cause of this shattering is the opening-up of a deeper center, a kind of bottoming-out, as if God had pulled the rug out from under us; we are left looking down into the bottomless depths of our nothingness, an inexplicable void. This is a terrible experience. The journey to the bottom is painful; we do not even want to look down—look within. But once we have gone all the way and discovered God at the bottom, we begin to enter into a new knowledge of God and self, and take on a new type of awareness or consciousness.

There is yet a third change in awareness I noticed, one which may or may not be connected with the two already mentioned. Prior to the night, I had always come up against a blank wall in my mind—it was the end of thinking. As a child I was convinced that if I could get to the other side of this wall, I might become a good thinker, a smart person. Somewhere in the dark night this wall disappeared and was never encountered again. My expectations of greater intelligence, however, did not come true. But if my mind was no better at scientific or mathematical thinking, I was nevertheless aware of having taken on a depth and dimension that went beyond thinking, a dimension that enabled me to see God in and through all things—nature, people, events, and so on. I saw how all thinking and reasoning went around in circles, and could never break out of these circles until it could get to the other side of the wall. My conclusion, therefore, was that the wall was the darkness of God Himself, Whose darkness one day gave way to light—which happened in the night.

Altogether, this new state of consciousness is such that when we reflect on our self or look inward, we always encounter God, which means there has been a shift from ordinary self-consciousness to a type of God-consciousness in which the object of consciousness is no longer just self, but also God. I always thought of this as a type of "we" or "us" consciousness, because I felt—I knew— that God and I were an unbeatable team, and though we never won a thing, we at least took the losses together, and in the end, when we lost everything, we even disappeared together.

In the unitive state, then, God has become not only the deepest experience of being or center of union, but also the primary object of reflective consciousness. During the night's acclimating process, we felt lost to our self as an object of consciousness, and the deepest feeling that remained was one of personal nothingness, wherein we could see nothing left to call a self. What emerges from this loss, however, is a self discoverable in God, a self that can no longer be known apart from Him. What is finally revealed, then, is the union of God and self, and with this revelation there is the beginning of a new life.

Some twenty-five years after this present transformation, I went through a further transformation, one more radical in that it did away with both the unitive center and the reflective mechanism of the mind—that is, both poles of consciousness. Because of the later transformation, I look back and see the basic incompleteness of the earlier experience in the Dark Night of the Spirit. In the earlier process, God seems to take over the objective pole of consciousness, the objective "me" or self-center—"ego-center," as some call it—yet he leaves intact the subjective, or "I," pole of consciousness. Thus in the unitive stage we have the union of subject and object, the I and Thou, and not separate identities. If the polar "I" were eclipsed, there could be no knowledge of unity, not even a knowledge of identity; for what would be left? As I see it, union is an imperative prerequisite for the later transformation or permanent suspension of the reflective "I" consciousness. With God as partner, we fulfill this earthly life and, in doing so, prepare for the next—a life of oneness beyond unity. This is like saying: before there is no-self, there must be self. Or, before no-union, there must be union.

In order to shortcut the contemplative journey, it may be tempting to think that we can do away with the unitive Self from the outset, since we must go beyond it in the long run. But such an attempt would only succeed in going beyond the ego-self in order to first come upon the true Self or union. Thus there is no short cut; I do not see the possibility of going beyond self unless our Partner in union makes this a reality.

What we have come to now, at this midpoint in our spiritual journey, is the end of the Dark Night of the Spirit. All parts of being and faculties of soul are conformed to the center of union and are functioning in the balance of their original design. Throughout the house there is great silence and stillness; from its innermost center, God reigns. At last we are whole, free, and poised, as it were, to experience the fullness of the unitive state.

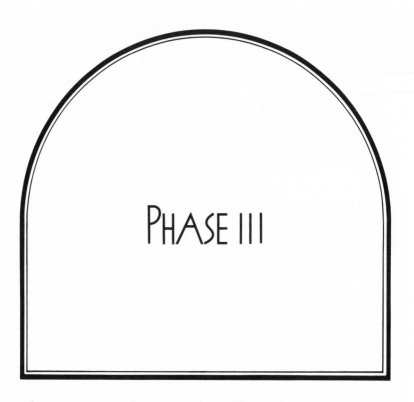

PHASE III

There are several reasons for calling Phase III a "peak phase" of the unitive life. One reason is that it marks the culmination of the transforming process and the onset of a new movement. Having arrived on top, there is the inevitability of a turning point. Because the contemplative life is a continuous movement, with no standing still, a new direction must now come into view. Thus, as the end of the old life and the beginning of the new, this phase has a dual but continuous movement. First, the soul is drawn inward to be absorbed, consumed, and inflamed; thereafter the movement turns outward with a powerful thrust from the center, to eventually move us out and beyond the self. If I could describe the dual aspect of this movement and how it comes about, I will have recaptured the essence of this period of the unitive life.

Another reason for calling this a peak phase is that it is the one point in the contemplative journey where, for a period of time, there seems to be nothing wanting, no more to be desired apart from the eternal vision. Thus, we come upon the full and cloudless enjoyment of the unitive state, where life is as perfect as it is ever going to be. At the same time, we are given glimpses of a state that lies ahead, which, from where we stand, appears to be heaven itself. So great are these advanced glimpses, and so great is the disparity revealed between this life and the next state, that we desire either to die or to have no more such glimpses. But, if not destined to move immediately into the next life, we must then be given a new direction in this one.

We left the last phase at a plateau of silence and darkness, which darkness now gives way to a light at the center. It is as if the strength and power of the center were openly manifesting itself and growing in intensity as a flame that melts and absorbs. So great is the magnetism of the center that the imperative need is to let go and sink in, to become lost in God. At times this need is so urgent and overwhelming we may find it difficult to concentrate on ordinary duties, and find ourselves forgetful and distracted. But once we sink in, we enter a state of complete forgetfulness, wherein the painless gaze absorbs our whole being in the depths of its objectless vision. At this time, any distinction between God and self is obliterated; the vision is all. Thus, the peak phase has a dual character: there is the potential for complete absorption— which I call "sinking in"—while the underlying state is the habitual awareness of this potential to sink in, or the awareness of the continuous magnetic drawing power of the center.

The habitual underlying state is similar to the prayer-of-quiet, wherein there is interior stillness as well as the consciousness of a deep abiding oneness with God; this state remains permanent throughout the unitive life. At this period, however, we come upon the ability to sink to yet a deeper level, similar to the prayer-of-union, wherein there is not only interior silence, but also silence of the mind, and in the clarity of this gaze, the self is lost from consciousness.

It is in the unitive center that the soul is indistinguishable from God, for outside this center all superficial aspects of self remain the same, and the mind, when not rapt in silence, is totally of the self. Thus, while all aspects of the self are conformed and unified around the center, they are clearly distinguishable from it—and God. It is only when sinking to the depths of vision that the mind and memory are absorbed, and the superficial aspects of self disappear from mind, and with the elimination of all boundaries, it is impossible to say where "I" leave off and God begins. Sinking, in, then, is the dissolution of the lines of separation between what is mine and what is Thine, but even here there is nothing in such an experience that would lead one to surmise or declare that "I am God" or "God is I," because all sense of "I" has disappeared. In the ordinary, underlying, habitual state, however, the "I" is only indistinguishable at the center, for outside the center—and especially in the mind—there remains full awareness of the distinction between I and Thou.

During this period, sinking in or the prayer of full union is not truly a transient experience or something that comes and goes; rather, we are now given the power to sink in any time we are free to do so—and may even sink in when not free to do so, for the magnetic pull to drop in is very great during this peak phase. But apart from the dual character of this period, there are also transient experiences—glimpses of a further state—and I have something to say about these later on.

What marks this stage, then, is the power of sinking in, a power which I, for one, had for over three years, until I gave it up of my own accord in order to move on. And what prompts or brings about this further movement will constitute the major turning point of the entire unitive life. Before accounting for this turning point, however, it may be of interest to stop and ask if the prayer-of-union (sinking in) can become the habitual, underlying state of the unitive life. Would it be possible to talk and work while in a state wherein the mind and memory are continually absorbed in silence? Could this become a permanent earthly state of existence? Or must we wait until heaven? St. John of the Cross, of course, tells us that the permanent suspension of the faculties in this life is not possible, and yet he does not say why. He simply takes this for granted, as in *Spiritual Canticle*, Stanza 26. I regard this assumption as a grave mistake, because down the road this type of consciousness does, in fact, become a great reality.

To begin with, there are subtle degrees of this full suspension, and in one of the lower, gentler degrees it is quite easy to work within this state. However, it must be work done in silence and solitude, work that needs little intellectual effort and almost no memory. It goes without saying that it would not be compatible within a socializing milieu where there is a lot of talk, and where tasks are intellectually, mentally absorbing. The continuous pull toward complete mental silence is too great for this; in fact, the nature of this pull becomes all the more insistent and pronounced when we try to go against it. It is like trying to swim against a powerful current: we finally become so exhausted that our energy gives way and we are forced to give up. At that point we must turn to go with the flow.

Here I think of the tales of the mystics who, it is said, fell into ecstasy in the middle of a conversation or some activity. Evidently they were going against the current until they came to a point where no further resistance was possible, and thereupon lapsed into mental silence—they had to give themselves up to it. They were not overpowered by anything said to them, but rather by what was not said to them—the Great Silence itself. This silence *is* the contemplative gaze. It is the seeing of the Unknown that absorbs the intellect, overpowers the mind, and brings it to a standstill.

Merely to look within and see God at the center is not the contemplative gaze; to look within, God is still object—although formless and obscure—whereas in the contemplative gaze God is, as it were, subject—because self-awareness is no longer possible and the awareness of God is all. This gaze is analogous to a blinding light that obliterates the sight of everything but itself; thus the light knows nothing outside itself and sees only itself. Although this "seeing" is an intense type of suspension, yet with a lesser degree it would be possible to live a life of silence and solitude and remain in this state. Why we do not hear from those who live this way is obvious: if they were to write, lecture, or speak to us about it, they would be stepping outside it—at least at this stage. But if this is not a permanent fixture of the unitive life, in the peak phase it is nevertheless within the contemplative's power to sink in whenever he desires or is free to do so; thus, in this phase, the contemplative lives on a fine line between two states.

At this juncture, I would point out that down the road—twenty years later—I discovered that this full unitive state—the continuous contemplative gaze—becomes a permanent state of affairs, which no activity can possibly alter. It seems that just as the prayer-of-quiet is the basic underlying state of the unitive life, so too, the prayer-of-union becomes the basic underlying state of the life beyond self and union. What is required, for this to happen, however, is a further change of consciousness, an irrevocable doing away with self-consciousness, and why it does not occur at this time, or during this particular phase of the unitive life, I am not sure. As already noted, those for whom it becomes a permanent state in this phase are never heard from, which does not mean it has not happened or cannot happen. These souls evidently do not write books or leave anything behind, and of those who do write, we hear nothing of such a happening. What we have to take for granted, then—in lieu of accounts to the contrary—is that full suspension of the faculties is not the permanent characteristic of the period following spiritual marriage or transforming union.

One suggestion to account for this is that, in the stages that lie ahead, the self is very much needed to withstand the challenges and tests that seem imperative to a forward movement. Full suspension of the faculties is a selfless state because self-consciousness is permanently suspended—held in silence. As a God-given survival mechanism, however, a premature loss of self-consciousness could prove overwhelming; we must first build up to its demise through the trials of the unitive life. As said before, without a fully tested trust in and abandonment to the unitive Partner, the unitive-self can never be wholly left behind, and later I hope to show how this works. For now, however, we are still acclimating to the full unitive state and beginning to discover some of its effects and graces.

The habitual, permanent state is deep and profound. It is as if in the deepest aspect of our being there is "something" solid, something that has a tight hold on our being, something that holds these depths in silence and stillness. At the same time, this interior hold is felt as a great strength, which we gradually recognize as a power or flame that burns intensely. This flame is born of stillness, and, as it emerges from the plateau of silence, it gathers intensity as if moving outward; it cannot be contained in so small a center, lest it consume us and we die. But the flame does not consume us. Rather, it lies within as a power, a strength, a burning love, a presence in itself, and the mainstay of our existence. Thus, as we are drawn inward to the flame we are, at the same time, thrust outward by it. This is not a passing experience, for the flame burns steadily and continuously throughout the rest of the unitive life.

The problem with the flame is what to do with it. If we sit still, it would consume us without dying, and if we move outward, we encounter the further problem of finding adequate expression for it. Thus comes the burning solution: to either die—to have eternal vision—or to move in order to return so great a love. It is to affirm and return God's love that the soul desires to endure every trial and suffering within human limits. At this time, for example, I envisioned for myself a walk through a snake- and malaria-infested jungle without a movement of hesitation, fear, or a single thought for the self. I wanted to do this not for God especially, and certainly not for myself, but simply to exercise this union, to put it on the line, because it is in the exercise of this union that its true glory breaks through and His face appears. And the tougher the exercise, the clearer the vision.

So the desire to suffer has nothing to do with the love of suffering. On the contrary, suffering is the road to bliss and, in the end, is bliss. At the same time, suffering and trials assuage the burning need to return love; that is, to contribute to this union, a contribution that can be nothing less than giving all—and more than all, by stretching the human limits whatever they be. For this reason I envisioned my life ahead as one of running the gauntlet, dangling over pits, walking a tightrope, sitting on Job's dung heap—not physical feats, of course, but anything that would try the spirit of love and trust to the nth degree. Looking back on these youthful desires, I now see they were prophetic, for in this respect all my desires were fulfilled. Yet always at the end of the rope His face would appear and once more I would be saved. St. John of the Cross says that at this stage the soul has such power with God that God fulfills its every desire, yet I think it is the other way around: God gives the soul the desires He intends to accomplish in it, come what may. This is the only way to account for the even match between our desires and their eventual reality; left to ourselves, we do not know the right things to ask of God. I am convinced God moves us forward by going contrary to every desire we think right, proper, correct, just, and necessary. When the peak phase is over, the contemplative moves forward like the salmon swims upstream. Going upstream is the most strenuous and difficult period of the salmon's life, and when it finally arrives at tranquil, peaceful waters, its destiny is fulfilled and the salmon dies. In the case of the contemplative, of course, it is the final remnant of self-awareness that dies.

Right now, however, we are still at the peak phase, gathering energy for the trek upstream. In this gathering of energy, the flame lights the way forward and generates the turning point—the outward thrust that moves us forward. At this point, I came upon an aspect of God I had never seen before, an aspect that would reinforce the forward movement.

What I saw was how God was the eternal movement, which meant more than that God moves; it also meant: this is *what* God is—namely, movement. Years before, I had seen God as Existence, and later, as Everywhere. And though there were other seeings in which the true nature of God was revealed, one thing they had in common was that they were apropos to the present state, wherein they acted as a light to the way forward. How I saw the eternal movement may have something in common with the experience of the apostles at the time of the Ascension. After Christ had disappeared into a cloud, they stood for a long time looking up; as I see it, he did not completely disappear, but continued to be seeable in a different, more obscure way. The apostles stood there, hardly able to believe this reality—stunned by the wonder of this new type of seeing. It took two angels to break their trance and indicate that they must move on, since they would again see Christ coming, and next time in glory. Thus the requisite for the vision of Tabor is not to stand still, but to keep moving.

Another connotation of the eternal movement was that, interiorly, the Holy Spirit was always in movement, always moving us toward our final destiny. The movement of transformation was now at an end, but since God has no end, the Spirit continues to move the soul forward to yet a further end. Thus I knew without doubt that there was something more down the road, something beyond this peak state. Yet to move forward was difficult because I could see no path. St. John of the Cross once drew a map of the spiritual life, which he depicted as the trek up Mount Carmel. At the top, the peak, he wrote: "Here there is no longer any way because for the just man there is no law, he is a law unto himself." This attests to the boundless freedom of the full unitive state and that the way forward is of man's own choosing; meaning, from here on there is no specific path, and man is on his own. Until this point, God has led us on a secure path, brought us the great freedom which derives from our union with Him, and now man must exercise this freedom, exercise the unitive life. This may sound easy to do, but in fact, nothing could be more difficult.

We do not know the way forward, and so much freedom boggles the mind and spirit; we have come upon nothing like it before. In vain we look for a secure path, and when it does not appear we sit down on the peak and do not take the initiative. It is all very risky. For myself, I stepped out with a rope attached—that is, cautiously. Then one day I was given the man-in-the-airplane treatment and was shoved out without any attachments. That there was no great splat attests to the miracle of the unitive state. It is like the butterfly emerging from the cocoon: there is fear and unknowing before it suddenly discovers it can fly, discovers that this is what its transformation was all about, and that to fly is the essence of its mature life.

So far, my concern has been to show how and why a turning point occurs at this peak stage, or how the movement of God draws us inward only to move us outward. This is not an intellectual movement or even one that makes sense. Rather, it is the movement of both a subtle power and an unknowable, unfathomable intelligence. No one else is moving in us; we only move at all because God moves us, for outside God no movement is possible. But in this movement we come upon many discoveries of how God works in us, what changes He has wrought, and what are the effects of the full unitive state. Although basically simple in itself, this state is difficult to convey, and usually results in sounding more complicated than it really is. Yet one could do nothing better with one's life than make the attempt to say something of this unitive gift of God.

One thing I learned was how the experience of life in the deepest center was greater than all previous contemplative experiences, greater than the sense of presence, infusions of love, feelings of peace, and so on. No feeling whatsoever could compare to the solid, intense, "seeing" type of life that lies at the deepest level of being. From this vantage point, all previous experiences were seen as superficial and deceptive in that I could now see there was always an element of self in them. I looked back and saw how self had its finger in every experience, thereby polluting it, and that as long as any self remained, there could be no pure experience of God. It is a rare thing, I think, to have an interior experience wherein self does not respond in some way, or get in the way. After seeing how this worked, I never again wanted any experience of God wherein self could either be seen or felt, and here I knew I was asking for some high experiences indeed. Yet if I could not have God pure and simple, without any admixture of self, then I wanted nothing at all. When we come to pure seeing, we will have nothing less; when we possess a beautiful gem we cannot become excited about a stone of lesser cut. God is greater than all experiences of Him, and now that we possess Him so surely and clearly, we can let our experiences go. Thus, seeing God at the bottom is the end of the experiential life; compared to this seeing, all former contemplative experiences now appear insipid. In other words, to possess God is sufficient unto itself and everything outside this possession is nothing.

With this insight, I felt I had come to a saturation point in my life of interior experiences. This point arose from the requirement to know God as He is in Himself without any mediumship or admixture of self; it was the experiential realization that God was beyond His gifts and graces, and that the closest one could come to pure experience of God was no experience; to possess Him was everything. God was the great reality seen in absolute silence and stillness; to have the vision stay, the self had to be equally in silence and stillness—to be no more, that is. God's immovable gift of Himself is the center, the strength, the power, the seeing, the flame that burns steadily. The very strength of this union is the ability to remain in this interior stillness and not move toward even the greatest of spiritual enticements—to take nothing from them.

I once told a friend that if I ever again experienced the presence of God, I would throw it away and run out and seek a distraction. She was as shocked and upset as if I had thrown God out of heaven; she did not understand I was only throwing away an experience of self. God is always bestowing His graces, but as long as self stands in the way, these graces are filtered through the self, distorted by the self, and, unwittingly, we end up loving our experiences—our self—and not God. How many people would spend their whole lives loving God if they never had a single experience of Him? It is unheard of. Fortunately, God does not ask us to do this; instead, He is tolerant of this thing called "self," working through it, around it and over it, until such time as we can live without it.

When I saw how self had kept me from pure vision, I decided it was better to spend the rest of my life in naked faith than ever again have an experience of God that was tainted with self, or have any experience that brought self-satisfaction. I was content to remain at the bottom where, in silence and stillness, the deepest aspect of self is indistinguishable from God, where self is forgotten and God is all. It was from this silence that a new life emerged, a new energy that, without any sweetness or delight, was the powerful flame of love, a flame that would never be extinguished until it had consumed its unitive partner, the self. I call this flame an energy because this is its experience. Initially I made the mistake of thinking this flame or energy belonged as equally to me as it did to God, but went on to make the bewildering discovery that I could never use it, tap into it, control it, increase or decrease it, express it in any way to the outside and, in the end, discovered it was not mine and never had been. Here in this phase, however, the flame has its origin. Born of the deep silence and stillness of God, its birth and rising up constitute the turning point in the unitive life.

Another finding at this time has reference to modifications of the emotional or affective system, and with regard to this, St. John of the Cross makes an interesting observation. He says that in the full unitive state the soul no longer feels compassion even though it does the works of compassion; it no longer feels grief or sorrow, nor do the "emotions of joy move the soul" anymore. He says the soul is too full, has reached its "full stature" or maturity, and no longer "grows through these new spiritual things as do others who have not arrived." These feelings, then, belong to a less mature stage; now, however, "the soul lacks what involved weakness in her practice of virtues, whereas the strength, constancy and perfection of them remains" (Stanza 21 S.C.). The weakness and imperfection in the practice of virtue was its emotional involvement, whereas true deeds of compassion or charity are devoid of all such movements. The soul now works from the true center of being, and not from the self's personal center, which is the emotions. Because emotions arise from the center of self, many people, I am afraid, have mistaken this for their true center of being, which, as we know, is God and therefore far removed from the emotional center.

True virtue does not arise from feelings, but from the strength at the center which needs no feeling to act. During the transformation, a shift occurred whereby acts are now either spontaneous—that is, they bypass both feeling and knowing—or arise from knowledge and no longer from feelings. St. John of the Cross compares this to the knowledge possessed by the angels "who judge perfectly the things that give sorrow without the feelings of sorrow," and "exercise the works of mercy without the feelings of compassion."

The discovery of this emotional modification came to me as a surprise. When situations arose that formerly would have called forth or aroused an emotional response, there occurred no change in the deep interior state, which remained imperturbably quiet. I thought this a wonderful grace and discovered it to be an unfailing protection. It was as if the interior flame acted as a burning sword standing before the door of the center, forbidding anything disruptive to enter. Again and again the door was buffeted, shaken and, at times, it seemed the whole world conspired to break it down; yet throughout the most tragic, frightening and awful situations, it never gave way. This was a wondrous thing; it was almost miraculous in its experience.

Despite its being an imperturbable state, St. John of the Cross has constant reference to the delights and joys of the unitive state, and thus his statements may appear to be in contradiction with what is said above. The unitive life is indeed a joyous state; even the lack of overt emotional joy is a joy. We have to understand, however, the difference between active emotional joy centered in the self, and a passive, infused type of joy derived from our true center, a joy that never exceeds its threshold—that is, never overflows to involve the emotions, senses, and lower aspects of self. Perhaps a comparison between active and passive joy will be of help in clarifying the difference.

Active emotions are specific, localized, and hopefully controllable. They stem from the mind—its desires, values, expectations, and all the rest. Passive feelings, on the other hand, are nonspecific, nonlocalized; they do not arise from the mind and are not under our control—in part, this is why infused graces are indescribable. In several passages St. John of the Cross compares this infusion to a breath or to breathing, which is an apt analogy since air is nonlocalized, does not arise from self, is not a feeling, has no boundaries, has no mental connection, and cannot be tangibly grasped. This breathing, he tells us, is God breathing in the soul in such a way that the soul's breathing seems to be God's breathing with no distinction between the two, and whatever we wish to call this—love, joy, bliss, peace—it belongs to both equally. This breathing is as far removed from emotionality as stillness is removed from rage. The emotions cannot enter into this infusion because they have no capacity to do so, they are without depth, have no access to the source, and are entirely of the self. Then too, God has no emotions. Too often we interpret the love felt by a beginner as the same love felt by the more proficient, when, in fact, a great transformation has taken place, a profound interior change that has matured us in every way. Thus love and joy, referred to in the beginning, are of an entirely different character later on. Only the words remain the same.

Perhaps a practical and personal example of how the affective system has been altered may be helpful here. At the same time, it may act to illustrate how things work in the unitive state.

I had been working side by side with an employer for over a year; we had a good rapport and, I thought, were good friends. One day in her absence I made a decision, one that turned out very well for everyone concerned. She said nothing about it. A month or so later she brought up this decision and told me I had overstepped my place in making it, and she did not stop there. In mounting tones of anger and nervousness, she verbally tore me apart and, as I watched, I saw her carried away by a powerful emotional force beyond herself, beyond all rational thought, beyond her normal behavior, and certainly beyond the situation itself. By the time she ended, I had been fired.

I watched this phenomenon in silence, without a thought for myself or any need to look within, yet I was aware that the center had risen to the top, come into full view, and its very appearance or presence was joy, a quiet, intense joy. Yet the first concern had been for my friend who was obviously unhappy. I would have liked to talk with her, but she would not allow a single word. In the years following I went to visit her several times to see if she was ready to make her peace with me, but she refused to speak. I could do no more for her and never went back again.

Hundreds of examples can be given of how the unitive state works; the point here is to show how it is a deeply joyful state, and in no way stoical or uncaring; indeed, when you are so well taken care of yourself, your first concern is for the other. It is a state that knows no anger, revenge, jealousy, greed and those hundred-and-one feelings indicative of self-centeredness. Sorrow, compassion, and charity are knowledgeable acts that do not derive from the emotions. At times there will be movements toward emotionality, but these movements do not go deep; they are somehow automatically checked by the center which is their threshold—a place they cannot enter. Nevertheless, the soul in this state can still suffer. It is a particular type of suffering, however, and I shall be speaking of this in the next phase. The soul can also be tried to the breaking point on every level of its existence, and this too will happen. Perhaps the only thing the soul is spared is the deep pain of the dark night, the extremes of emotionality, and most of the movements toward the extreme. Thus, the effective system is still alive, only it has been greatly modified.

Perhaps the word that most characterizes this state is "strength," a continuous, passively felt, interior strength at the center. In this strength lies all virtues; indeed, this strength is virtue. But the virtue we knew and practiced before is not the virtue we know and practice now. Previously, virtue was an activity, a discipline, a determination, a sacrifice, or something we do. But now virtue is primarily passive because the interior strength (or virtue) is the fusion of our deepest will to God, and its primary exercise is simply to remain in the unitive center—come what may.

Thus we stand strong in the midst of all external circumstances that would otherwise break us down or move us from the center. Without doing anything other than remaining silently in the center, the soul keeps its peace, its oneness with God, and exercises patience, long-suffering, trust, abandonment, and much more. Since all acts now stem from the true center (God) and not from the false center (the emotions), all acts are passive to God. On the outside, we may do what we can to rectify or alleviate unpleasant circumstances; yet virtue does not lie in what we do, but in the interior stance—that of standing strong in God. In the unitive life this stance becomes the soul's very nature—it knows no other way of life; it is the deepest habit of soul, a habit that goes on whether we are aware of it or not. We cannot help but live with God; the matter has gone beyond all possibility of choice.

In order to keep this unity at the forefront of consciousness, the soul has what amounts to a passion for the exercise of its unitive strength, and for this reason welcomes every trial and tribulation—at least before-hand. The greater the trial, the greater the exercise of strength (virtue), and the greater the awareness of unity—this is the way it goes. Some trials only demand patience and calmness, while others demand everything in the books, and then some. There may be trials of long dura-tion, calling forth virtue so continuously that we may be wearied to the breaking point and feel our whole unitive life is on the line. When these trials are resolved and the burden is relieved, however, we find little contentment in the easy life, and begin looking forward to more tests, especially new ones that will tap into a different level of existence. In this way, we grow so accustomed to the dif-ficult life that we feel lost when things go right. At any rate, I believe the exercise of unitive strength, or virtue, to be a requirement of this state.

It has occurred to me that souls in this state who live a quiet, reclusive, secure way of life have little occasion for exercising this state and little variety in doing so; thus they are less aware of its benefits and, at times, may not be aware that they are in this state at all. For these souls, the state is less defined, less explored, less exercised, and never realized for its unique toughness and miraculous qualities. In other words, the unitive state does not show up for what it really is, and though many souls come to this state, they do not recognize it, cannot identify with it, and have few glimpses of its reality. Trials alone are the vehicle of unity's revelation, so much so that the most terrible of human trials is the herald of the greatest of human relevations—the pure vision that lies behind the door of the center. By "door" I mean the obscure seeing of God which gives way—opens up to clear vision.

Another aspect of this state is the blossoming of crea-tivity that is born of the fullness of this state and its need for expression. With all its freedom, new depths, and in-sight, the soul has a new eye on the world and no timidity with regard to expressing it. But if the state is original, creative, and innovative, the problem lies in finding an adequate outlet. For myself, I never found any creative satisfaction, but then I was not a particularly creative or talented individual to begin with. If anything, my talent was botching everything to which I put my hand while managing to muddle through and, by the grace of God, land on my feet. But since I was not allowed an ounce of creative success, I am not the one to expand on the creative aspects of the state; yet I know creativity is a part of the unitive life deriving from the inner benefits of the state, and not necessarily from any native talent.

So far we have been going over some of the properties of the unitive state that are discoverable in this peak phase. We learned that seeing into the depth of the center surpasses all former experiences, experiences in which self obviously had its finger; we put these experiences behind us because, from here on, the sole desire is to see God without any admixture of self. We said something about the modification of the affective system, and how clarity of mind takes precedence, so that doing stems from knowing and seeing, not from feeling. This is the result of becoming established in our true center (God), and having put behind us the false center (emotions). The turning point of the unitive life is the emergence of the flame, or great energy, at the center, which is not only the source of virtue, but virtue itself. To reveal the full strength of this union—the soul's cementedness to God—there is need of continual trials and tests of every kind, because from this exercise arises the revelation of "that" which lies behind the door at the center.

Although there are more discoveries to be recorded, I will pick up some of these as we go along, more especially in the next phase where "exercise is all." For now, I will turn to St. John of the Cross and point out those aspects of the full unitive state that I believe are important to bring forward. Since he has more to say about the full unitive life than any other saint, mystic, or contemplative writer in history, I could never hope to point out every-thing, or even do justice to what I select. There is, of course, no substitution for a complete reading or a one-to-one study of the saint's works.

As we turn to what he has to say, it might be well to begin with a few preliminary remarks. First, if the con-templative finds it difficult to identify with the lofty view and glowing account of the unitive life given by the saint, the reason is that his writing is heavily weighted in this direction, rather than in the direction of its more stable, practical, long-term effects and benefits. Thus he appears strained to the heights, as one who has no great distance on the experiences he describes. Then too, it must be re-membered he is not describing his personal experiences alone, but those he gleaned from a variety of sources.

Apart from his own life, as spiritual director he was acquainted with the experiences of others; he was a stu-dent of theology and scripture, and had read the mystics. Also, he writes from a long tradition, in particular from a point of view that regards the unitive stage as the highest attainable in this life. When, therefore, he speaks of the soul's great perfection, invincible virtue, and glorious dei-fication, he speaks as an outside witness, a scholar, poet, and writer, which is not necessarily representative of the soul's actual feelings about itself; indeed, the soul is not enamored with itself. After the dark night, there is never again a single doubt about its worthlessness and poverty; the soul knows well that God is its only adornment, and that its strength, goodness, and beauty are Him alone. The saint reminds us of this: "that the property of perfect love is to be unwilling to take anything for self, nor does it attribute anything to self, but all to the Beloved" (*Spir-itual Canticle*, Stanza 32). Thus we must reconcile his lofty view of this state by keeping in perspective how the soul sees itself, and how St. John of the Cross sees those souls who come to this peak stage.

Apart from being a recapitulation of previous states,

the primary concern of *The Living Flame of Love* is the description of transient experiences that mark this period of the journey. These experiences are important as fore-tastes and glimpses of a future state, but one that the saint felt could be realized only in the next life. As someone particularly interested in this future state, I shall return to these experiences, but only after pointing out the more stable, underlying elements of this present phase; for this, the *Spiritual Canticle* is the preferred book. From Stanza 22 to the end, the book covers the period of spiritual marriage and beyond. I cannot point out everything, but will emphasize those aspects I see as having the most long-term effects.

First of all, we are told that the unitive state is a habitual state of "deep tranquility, peace and unchanging good" where there is a "continuous loving attentiveness of the will to God." In its first movements, the soul is now inclined to God in so habitual a manner that it is often working for God "without thinking or being aware she is doing so" (Stanza 28)—that is, the soul now works from the center, of which it has continuous passive awareness, and no longer is aware of God by way of mental effort or active maintenance. It is as if we had to forget God to be aware of God in a more subjective manner.

In this state, the soul "resembles Adam in the state of innocence," because it knows and sees no evil "nor judges anything in a bad light, for she no longer has within her the habit of evil by which to judge them" (Stanza 36). This is a true and astute observation, and I would suggest several reasons why this soul is a poor judge of evil. To begin with, she now sees God in other people, sees the best in them, and is saddened when others go against their own best interests—the great good in themselves. Instead of evil, what she sees is ignorance, blindness, and spiritual immaturity—which, I might add, is in accord with what Christ said of those who killed him: "They know not what they do." In some ways, the inability to judge evil places this soul in a vulnerable position when dealing with worldly people. It is one reason she will have to suffer much from others and will, in fact, be destined a victim. Her trust in the goodness of others will continually be betrayed; they will take advantage of her goodness and virtue, which will be construed as naive weakness. Because this soul has depth and insight, she is sensitive to others and will therefore suffer far more than those who do not possess such sensitivity. This suffering, however, is all part and parcel of the way forward.

Another aspect of this state of innocence stems from the "new knowledge" given her, wherein she is incapable of seeing anything happening in her life that is not the will of God, or not in His plan for her; thus nothing that comes to her is evil. This knowledge is derived from the deep abiding assurance of the continued oneness of her will with the will of God. The marvel of this acceptance is that it is active, and takes suffering and whatever else comes without running away, or refusing a thing. Instead of curtailing personal initiative, seeing everything as God's will makes these souls "daring and determined in all their works" (Stanza 29). When there is failure, or things go wrong, these souls invariably land on their feet. This is a state of the undauntable spirit.

St. John of the Cross calls this state of innocence the "original state of unknowing"—unknowing as to the ways of the world, yet a blessed unknowing as to the ways of God. He points out, however, that "acquired knowledge of the sciences is not lost, rather it is perfected by the supernatural knowledge infused into the soul, as when a faint light mingles with a bright light, the bright light prevails" (Stanza 26). This mingling of natural and supernatural knowledge is responsible for making those who reach this state appear brighter and more intelligent than they would otherwise appear on a purely academic scale of measurement. Intelligence soars in this state, and even where it may be natively lacking, it will be filled in, expanded, and enhanced by supernatural illumination. It is the divine light that gives the soul depth of insight and originality—a seeing beyond what is obvious or apparent.

If we put this enlightened intelligence together with the enhanced talents and creativity of the state, we might expect the emergence of an extraordinary individual—a fact attested to by many saints and mystics who took nothing from the university. But in reality, the soul has only attained to its "full stature" and maturity as a human being; it has only become what it was meant to be in the first place. In other words, the transformation has normalized and matured the soul, put it in line with God's original design and, therefore, is no more and no less than what it was from the beginning—but a common human being.

The irony, however, is that when placed among the so-called normal people of this world these souls will appear as odd fellows. St. John of the Cross calls attention to this fact when he says the world criticizes those who are given entirely to God. The world thinks them "excessive in their conduct, estranged and withdrawn, and asserts that they are useless in important matters and lost to what the world esteems" (Stanza 29). I find this a valid criticism; these people do not fit into society and, like Christ, down the road they will pay the price.

Although the saint makes frequent reference to the soul's deification, he reminds us in Stanza 26 that deification refers only to the innermost center, "and not as though on the surface, but in the interior of her spirit." On the surface of things little has changed; the transformation is not concerned with external features. The unitive state wears no particular face to the world; there is no uniform mold to which the soul conforms after its transformation. Only God and the soul know of this interior state; nothing appears of it on the outside. Some transformed souls will be likeable and others will not, but one thing they have in common is that they do not care if they are liked or not. These souls, we are told, execute their works "without thought of what others will say or how their work will appear," and the saint adds, "few spiritual persons reach such daring and determination in their works" (Stanza 29). Few, that is, dare to be themselves without putting on roles or playing social games. What the deified soul is, then, is a soul that is authentic, whole, natural, spontaneous, fearless, and strongly itself in every event and situation. God has not fashioned a wimp, weasel, or robot.

I think St. John of the Cross goes out on a limb when he says that, because the soul is deified or one with God, all its works are now divine. What is divine is the deep, interior source of acts, not the acts themselves. On the surface, there is nothing divine about nursing the sick, peeling carrots, or even praying. Nor does a good intention make an act divine. The saint is speaking about the central wellspring from which our acts derive; for, as I have said, the overriding awareness of the unitive life is that the soul, at the deepest level of its being, is one with God, and it now acts and lives from this depth. It is a very unified, strong feeling to act from this center, but it does not insure that our acts are always correct, or that the mind is no longer subject to faulty judgment. At times, when we can act under the influence of infused love, our acts have an air of the divine, but even then, I find it difficult to claim any divinity for them. To me, a divine act only occurs when the soul does nothing, and God acts through it without her knowing or cooperation. In a push-and-shove crowd, Christ suddenly turned and asked, "Who touched me?" Without his knowledge or initial consent, power went out from him. This is an amazing mediumship, a truly divine act.

Indicative of the unitive state is the continual awareness of the soul's central strength, about which the saint has much to say. In a number of places, the symbol he uses for this strength is the "single hair" which signifies the singleness of the unitive will-to-God; in Stanza 31, he couples this with the singleness of the "eye," which is characteristic of the single-mindedness (continuous awareness) of the state. Together, the single hair and eye denote the soul's "union with God in the intellect and will. Faith and fidelity signified by the eye, resides in the intellect; and love, signified by the hair, resides in the will." What is more, this single strand of hair is the strength of love which "binds the virtues together in such a way that if it breaks where one of these virtues lies it will immediately fail in regard to them all." That to fail in one is to fail in them all is reminiscent of the all-or-none law which attests to the tightness and indissolubility of the unitive bond. This is obviously not a state of tension between self and God, or self and the world; it is not a state of compromise, mere balance, or the reconciliation of opposites; all-or-none means we are either one with God all the time or not one with Him at all. It means that the soul lives with the fullest degree of intensity wherein there is no grading of interior strength or unity. We cannot be more unified or less unified; rather, this oneness with God is all-or-none, and to live life at the fullest possible degree of intensity is another characteristic of the unitive life.

No doubt it was due to this indissoluble bond that the saint believes that the soul in this state is confirmed in grace; that is, because the soul is so tightly bonded to God, it can no longer go against God (Stanza 22). Should this hair or strength of bond be broken, the unitive state would unravel backward through the transforming process like a butterfly reverting back through the cocoon to the larva stage. I do not see this happening, and perhaps the marvel of this state is that it does not happen. If this state were dependent upon the soul holding this unity together or having to maintain it, it would certainly fall apart. The strength and fidelity of this union comes only from God, and that it does not come unbound is due to his pledge to the soul. This is the very meaning of spiritual marriage: there is no going back, no undoing of what has been done. The soul shares in the divine life; it claims none of it as its own, because in itself the soul remains as before—good for nothing.

It is God's pledge and fidelity that liberates the soul, gives it freedom, confidence, security, and independence. But in the exercise of these gifts, God is always saving the soul—rescuing His partner. To have this saving experience, however, the soul has to live fully and intensely, to take all the risks—come to the end of its rope, crawl out on limbs, and reach the threshold of the breaking point, even risk having its union fall apart. Otherwise it can never realize the enduring love and fidelity of God, and what it means to be confirmed in His saving grace. Those who live in fear and trepidation of falling, sinning, losing ground—who spend their lives making sure they do not—have little trust in God and do not exercise the gifts of the unitive state, and because they never experience the continual saving grace of this state, would have no understanding of what it means to be confirmed in grace. But then, failure to take risks is not indicative of the unitive life.

As a theological question, confirmation in grace is thought to mean that the soul can no longer sin or offend God, but, in truth, there is no use counting on the soul for any such thing. There is no true equality in this kind of marriage; in this marriage the husband is always saving the wife, picking up the pieces, righting the wrongs, and every day starting all over again. In practical detail, it is almost a comic state. Increasingly, the soul becomes less and less necessary for this union, and God becomes increasingly all in all until, finally, the soul realizes the truth of what the saint says of this state: "The two wills are so united that there is only one will and one love—which is God's" (Stanza 38).

A marriage that may have begun on the note of "we"

or "us" gradually dissolves until there is no "I," and God is all that remains. This gradual unmasking of the self, however, is a progressive revelation because man cannot afford to lose his unitive self overnight; the very nature and purpose of the unitive state is to bring about this final demise of the self; it is all a preparation for a more final transformation. But unless we are confirmed in grace, unless we realize by experience that God will never let us go, we cannot let go of the self. It is as if God had to prove to us again and again that, when all is gone, He still remains. The way forward, then, is to exercise the great gifts of the unitive life, to take all the risks, stretch the human potential, and allow God to save us every day, every moment of our lives.

The way forward is clearly defined in Stanza 36, wherein the soul desires to enter more fully into the "thicket" or fullness of God. To do so, the soul would suffer a "multitude of trials and tribulations," because it is "the means of penetrating further, deep into the thicket of the delectable wisdom of God." Since this is the key to a whole new direction, one passage from Stanza 36 is worth quoting in full.

A soul with an authentic desire for divine wisdom wants suffering first, in order to enter this wisdom by the thicket of the cross! Accordingly, S. Paul admonished the Ephesians not to grow weak in their tribulations and to be strong and rooted in charity in order to comprehend with all the saints what is the breadth and height and depth, and to know also the supereminent charity of the knowledge of Christ, in order to be filled with all the fullness of God. The gate entering into these thickets of His wisdom is the cross which is narrow and few desire to enter by it, but many desire the delights obtained from entering here.

Charity, then, is the way forward, and charity by its very nature means suffering, because it means giving of the self. Partnership with God enables the soul to give to the last farthing because, apart from God, the soul has not a thing to lose. This particular giving (suffering) is accompanied by a deep joy, not a superficial, emotional joy, but the joy of having God constantly before our eyes; compared to this, there is no other joy in the unitive life. Indeed, all else is but toil and trouble. For the remainder of the unitive life, this charity or selfless giving will be the direction, the emphasis, and the gauge of divine love; by this alone can it enter further into the depths of God.

But this is not the only reason the soul desires to suffer. The burning desire of this phase, and the fountain-head of charity, is to love God as equally as God loves the soul, to give as it has received, to return measure for measure, "for the lover cannot be satisfied if he fails to feel that he loves as much as he is loved," "nor would he be satisfied in heaven if he did not feel he loved God as much as He loves him." Thus, to return love, the soul would go through every test, forfeit every experience, prove its love by suffering, and spend the rest of its life giving without receiving a thing in return—to such lengths is the soul carried away in its desire to return love for love. This desire for equality of love is a particular problem in this peak stage, and a difficult one to solve; in fact, it is so difficult, I am convinced that it cannot be solved at all. St. John of the Cross offers a number of solutions, such as the following:

God loves nothing outside Himself. He bears no lower love for anything than the love He bears for Himself. He does not love things because of what they are in themselves, but because of what He is in Himself . . . With God, to love the soul is to put her somehow in Himself and make her His equal. Thus He loves the soul within Himself, with Himself, that is, with the very love by which He loves Himself.

—*Stanza 32.*

To understand this type of equality, we have to see that for God to love us is the same as for God to love Himself, and that the love the soul bears for God is God's own love. Thus it is not "I" who love God; rather, it is God loving himself. In other words, what God loves in me is Himself, and "that" in me which loves God, is also Himself. To completely realize the truth of this insight comes very close to doing away with the self altogether, for if "I" do not love God, then what good am I? How am I needed or necessary? The day we see the full implication of what this means, we are getting close to the final demise of the self; with this demise, there is no union remaining, and therefore no further need for equality of love. Thus, one way out of the problem of equality of love is to have no equality at all. God loving Himself is the only equality there is.

The reason it is not possible, I think, to do without the unitive-self at this stage is that we have yet to really discover it; this is done in the exercise of the particular gifts of the unitive life, or when we move beyond this stage to love fully and fearlessly. When first arriving on this peak, we cannot distinguish in our deepest center the true self from God. What allows us to know that the self remains is everything outside this center—body, mind, feelings, consciousness itself—all those parts now unified around the center which are not, however, the center itself. That aspect of self bound to God in the center is the will-to-God, while all other aspects that radiate from this center are more superficial, perhaps, but self just the same. Transient experiences in which there is complete loss of all sense of self are prevalent at this peak stage; why contemplative authors do not see no-self as a future state is unknown. Like everyone else, I too did not suspect it; I could not see the possibility of getting through the practical affairs of life in such a marvelous state, which, I might add, is far more than simply the loss of self. Even had I been told that this state was possible in

104

this life, I would not have had the slightest idea how to make it happen or how to get there. St. John of the Cross says well, "Here there is no way," meaning that we do not know what is down the road; there seems to be no path.

In another place the saint does away with the problem of equality of love by saying that God wants nothing from the soul, since it can give Him nothing He does not have already. God only wants to glorify the soul, and letting Him do this is all the soul can give. But this solution ignores the fact that the automatic, spontaneous response of the self to God's love is the desire to return in equal measure. The self knows its love is no match for God's love, and the recognition of this truth is the impasse that constitutes the turning point of the unitive life. Up to this point, the transformation process was entirely God's doing, but now the direction changes and the soul will have its chance to do—to give to the last drop. The problem, then, is resolved when the soul turns to go with the outward thrust of the interior movement, go out beyond the self because of a love it cannot contain.

This new direction is verified in Stanza 38, where we are told that the soul's two great desires at this time are: to receive "essential glory"—that is, to see God face-to-face—and to give love. He explains why, at this point, the desire to give is greater than the desire to receive.

Just as the ultimate reason for everything is love (which is seated in the will), whose property is to give and not to receive, whereas the property of the intellect (which is the subject of essential glory) lies in receiving and not giving, the soul in the inebriation of love does not put first the glory she will receive from God, but rather puts first the surrender of herself to Him through true love, without concern for her own profit.

Since the vision, which presupposes the fullness of love, can be received only in the next life, the soul's first desire is to give love. Thus giving, or love, takes precedence in the unitive state, just as vision or receiving takes precedence in the next state—the state beyond union.

In this stanza the saint already envisions the life ahead and tells us that we proceed toward it by way of giving—charity. To attain the vision, however, we need not be dead; man is *in* the body but not *of* the body, and what can be glimpsed in the flesh can be realized in the flesh. If this were not true, no one would be around to tell us about it. God or heaven is not in some far-off place; to see God we need not go anywhere or move at all. To see God we need only be prepared, and this preparation is what the unitive life is about.

In his commentary on "the flame that consumes and gives no pain," we are told something of the "new transformation" that lies ahead. Although in this present state of union

there is conformity, still the soul suffers some degree of pain and detriment; first because of the beatific transformation which the spirit lacks; and secondly, because of the detriment which is suffered by weak and corruptible sense from its contact with the fortitude and loftiness of love that is so great.

—*Stanza 39.*

What is obviously wanting from this present unitive state is the vision, and the ability to contain so great a love. This tells us in what way the unitive state is incomplete, imperfect, and how there lies ahead a more complete and perfect transformation, one which "is not like that which the soul experienced in this life."

The reason our present transformation is imperfect, he says, is that although the coal and fire (the soul and

God) are one, the "fire nevertheless reduces the coal to ashes." In other words, because there is no true equality of love between self and God, the self is eventually reduced to an ash heap; the weaker partner is consumed by the flame, and when there is nothing left to consume, even the fire goes out. This is exactly what happens down the road; it is the most succinct explanation of the unitive life I know of. It also explains how and why we come to a later transformation: there has never been any equality in this union. Indeed, the reduction of the unitive self to an ash heap is the perfect fulfillment of the unitive life. But when there is nothing left, from the ash heap of "what was" arises the great vision of "what is." To bear the vision, however, the saint says God will have to "somehow strengthen" and equip the soul, give it the necessary capacity and fortitude—stretch the human limits, that is. The self, however, was that which created a boundary, that which was bound, that which could be fortified and stretched. But without a self there is only the Limitless— the Infinite.

Stanzas 38 and 39, which I have been referring to, are descriptions of transient experiences. In part, their importance is to set off by sheer contrast those elements in the unitive life that are still wanting and imperfect; also, they act as indicators of a further state. They are important learning devices because their loftiness engenders the impetus and generosity that propels the soul forward. These experiences serve a great purpose; they are not rewards or sweeteners, but rather glimpses of the Truth, the revelation of man's potential for the divine, for knowing God ever more perfectly—knowing Him as He knows Himself.

It is difficult to understand why we cannot foresee that these experiences indicate possibilities for this life. Prior to this time, all such experiences or foretastes were understood as heralds of a more advanced state to be known in the here and now. Prayer-of-quiet and union, the dark night, and all experiences prior to spiritual marriage were previews and preparations for a further state, yet in this peak phase we somehow regard these glimpses as belonging to a beatific or heavenly existence. Needless to say, it does not follow.

For myself, these advanced glimpses indicated that what was wanting from pure vision was a permanent loss of self—or everything I experienced that could be called a self. Still, I too could not see how it could come about in this earthly condition. But of one thing I was sure: there had to be more to the contemplative life than transformation and spiritual marriage; man could certainly know more of God than this. I intuited that something more lay down the road and, though I did not know what it was, I was willing to give up everything to find it. In this, I was not to be disappointed.

I cannot say why others who come this far do not share the intuition of a further state beyond union. Possibly it is due to the sense of fullness in this peak phase; the sense of having gone as far as possible in one direction, as well as the knowledge that the transformation is over.* Then too, the habitual, underlying unitive state is a great thing in itself; apart from the desire for eternal vision and the need to give as we have received, there is deep joy and peace. Compared to the dark night, this new state strikes us as a piece of heaven already. Perhaps it is this sense of fullness and lack of distance that makes us think these foretastes pertain to the next life; after all, they seem to point to something far ahead and we see no way there, nor can we imagine what is left to be transformed. Thus on the peak there is a certain sense of attainment. From here on the way forward is one of blind

---

* St. John of the Cross attests to this sense of completion. See Stanzas 20–21.

trust in God. But this is easy; the dark night has proven to us that we never trust God in vain.

If St. John of the Cross did not foresee a later transformation in this living state, he must still be given credit for saying more about it than any other contemplative author. What *The Living Flame of Love* adds to his other works is the description of various transient experiences which, if they were to become permanent, would give us a picture of this later state. Although outlining this state might be a worthy project, it is not to the purpose of this book, which is primarily concerned with how to get there.

I think it fitting, however, to end this chapter by taking a look at the final experience recorded in *The Living Flame*. It is not only the last in the book, but the last experience the saint was to record; it might well have been his final word on the contemplative life. The experience I speak of is called the "awakening," which is the vision of God "as He is" and is part of the commentary on the verse "You awake in my heart." He tells us that although there are numerous awakenings, this one is the greatest. The remarkable aspect of this vision is seeing how God moves all things and, at the same time, how all things move in God, and because of this "common movement," all seems to be God. Earlier it was seen how God was the immanent moving force in all that is created, but here the soul sees something more: it sees how all things live and move and have their being in God, so that between the created and uncreated there is oneness of movement and existence. He says of this awakening:

And although it is true that the soul is now able to see that these things are distinct from God, inasmuch as they have created being, and it sees them in Him with their force, root and strength, it knows equally that God in His own Being is all these things in an infinite and pre-eminent way, *to such a point that it under-stands them better in His being than in themselves. And this is the great delight of this awakening.*

—Living Flame, *trans. Peers.*

Here we see the created within the uncreated as nei-ther separate nor apart; rather, they are one and move as one. While the created is not the uncreated, nevertheless God seems to be both, because the created is in Him and one with Him. God is the unmoved mover, for, though "God does not move," yet the "soul is enabled to see God is always moving," containing all within Himself "so that all things move in God and with God." He compares this unison of movement to an earthquake when "at the movement of the earth all material things in it move as though they were nothing." It is as if the created were but specks of dust within the vastness of the Creator, all mov-ing within the great flow of the eternal movement.

The apparent movement on the part of God strikes the saint as a wondrous and inexplicable thing, since "God moves not." The movement of God, however, is His interior movement of creativity and acts. Since nothing exists outside God, there is no place for God to move to, no place to go where He is not already; thus God is not moving around, coming and going; He is not in some far-off heaven, but is always here—everywhere—and we are in Him; He does not move. In God, however, we move because God moves us and the saint calls this movement the "awakening," and marvels at the fact that this awak-ening seems to be God, while, at the same time, it is our-selves.

From this it would seem that God has a threefold movement: within Himself he moves to act, create and sustain; within His creation He lives and moves as its life force, and in turn, His creation all moves in Him. Thus God is the unmoved mover and we, the moved.

But how is it possible, the saint asks, "for the soul to bear so violent a communication while in the weakness of the flesh?" He answers that God "protects its nature" and fortifies the soul in such a way that

the soul knows not if it be in the body or out of the body. This may easily be done by that God who protected Moses with His right hand.

Evidently the requirement to bear the vision is a sense of formlessness or bodilessness which does, in fact, characterize the later transformation and become a permanent state of affairs. (How this works I have written of in *The Experience of No-Self*. That St. John of the Cross says "this may easily be done" not only attests to this possibility, but indicates that it is a snap. The truth is: this vision rises from the ash heap of a self-that-was; it is an awakening of such a nature that the soul never again sleeps.

It is fitting that St. John of the Cross leaves the final experience of *The Living Flame* without description. This is the "breathing of God Himself into the soul" for which he feels no description can do justice, no description is possible. But from the *Spiritual Canticle* (Stanza 39) we know that, in this breathing, the soul cannot distinguish its own breath from that of God. And when our breathing is no longer our own, there is the final collapse of all duality, and the collapse of all words. Having run out of breath, as it were, what remains is the breath of God, which is silence. And so does this greatest of contemplatives end his work with a breath, a silence, which is his final statement to us all.

BETWEEN PHASES III AND IV

Having seen clearly that pure vision lies beyond all self-involvement—beyond the faculties of soul, feelings, responses, and even the door at the center—all former contemplative experiences now appeared less pure, tainted by contrast. For this reason, I decided if I could not at this time have the continual vision of God beyond self-consciousness, then I wanted no experiences at all; once the self is seen through—and beyond—nothing less than pure vision can entice. Like everyone else, I took it for granted that the permanent vision of God was reserved for the next life. And since I was not destined to die immediately, what I had to do now was to accept this present life—self included—and make the best of it. I was therefore willing to put my experiential life behind and move forward by way of simple faith; I now saw that faith devoid of all experience was the closest one could come to the truth, the reality of God. If self invariably had its finger in every experience, at least it could not touch naked faith, or faith that is utterly selfless.

This is a particular type of faith. It is not an intellectual assent to belief or a system of thought; it is not a faith that gives rise to feelings and experiences; it is not a mental construct we cling to with persistent will; rather, this faith is the truth of God as He is in Himself and not as He is in "my" self; it is a faith that comes *after* seeing and not before. Where, before transformation, faith was dependent upon our minds, wills, experiences—our self, that is—now, after transformation, faith or the truth of God never depends on anything outside itself.

What is more, because it is a realized truth, it is a faith we cannot live without even if we wanted to, even if we tried to run from it all the days of our lives. As long as faith rests with the intellect, we will always be subject to doubt and disbelief—after all, it is the nature of the intellect to doubt. This tells us we must go beyond the intellect if we are to lay hold of truth, and this laying-hold is what I regard as mature faith. In a word: faith is selfless, whereas our experiences and our knowledge are not.

When I first glimpsed the true beauty and meaning of a naked, selfless faith, I had the feeling of having come full circle in that, after the transformation, I was now back where I started—a most ordinary person of simple faith. The only difference was that I now had the faith of the butterfly and not of the caterpillar; a mature faith derived from seeing, experiencing, and transformation, which was now free from self and in no way dependent upon it. This faith, then, is the continuous, obscure seeing of truth, the vision that lies behind the door at the center, a vision obscured in this life by the self, but in the next, is beyond it.

Due to the realization that the possession of God in naked faith was superior to all experiences of Him in which self invariably had a hand, I was able to go beyond the honeymoon or peak phase of the unitive life. With no more taste for experiences, I prepared to fly—that is, to accept the mature life of this human adventure and take the leap into the unknown where "there is no longer any way." Initially, I jumped off with strings attached, and therefore may never have honestly accepted this mature life had not God, in one of those contemplative milestones, cut the strings and given me insight into a new dimension of the unitive life.

This milestone occurred one evening as I was about to fall asleep. As usual, I had sunk into the silent center and focused my gaze on God, when suddenly I was alerted by an unusual movement, a movement that somehow told me my time had come. While I was willing to give up all experiences in order to have pure vision, I was not sure how God would respond to this piece of generosity; after all, how much experience could I live without? In high moments, generosity knows no bounds, but at other times there is a tendency to compromise; thus I was skeptical of how things would go. But with the sudden movement at the center, I instinctively knew I was about to find out. The movement alerted me to watch carefully. With my eyes riveted on God, He slowly began to recede, fading to a mere pinpoint of light. Not wanting to lose the last vestige of vision, I remained for a long time intensely watching, hardly daring to breathe.

This was the third time in my life that God seemed to disappear. The first time I was nine years old, and the experience was the most devastating of my life; it took a miracle to save me. The second time was the entrance into the Dark Night of the Spirit recorded herein, which, despite the pain, I was able to take in stride. Here now is the third time.

Whether from shock or disbelief, I watched this disappearance in complete stillness, without a single response. It was a long time before it dawned on me that God had not really disappeared, but instead had only gone underground, and remained as a pinpoint of light. It was like the discovery of being able to see in the dark. After this, however, the point of light seemed to explode and become all of this human form but the external husk. I saw how God was indeed my very life and breath, and that Christ, as the true self, was the inner strength, the will-to-God, the essence of the new man—the butterfly itself. Obviously God had only withdrawn Himself as an interior object of vision in order to reveal Himself on yet a more subjective, everyday level. At the same time, it was clear that the true nature of all dark nights is God's moving progressively underground in order to take over our deepest subjective experience of personal being; this is how transformation works.

This experience had particular meaning because it verified a long-held intuition that Christ, who all my life had consistently refused to be an object of mind or feelings, was, like grace, too subjective to be objectified. When the pinpoint of light, the Holy Spirit, exploded outward, Christ was revealed as the true subjective self, the vessel whose center was the Spirit, the Spirit which remained as the object of interior vision—Christ's own vision. This told me that "that" in me which saw, knew, and loved God, and was one with Him, was Christ, the true subjective self.

Apart from its revelation, Christ's subjectivity is difficult to realize on an intellectual level; this is because Christ, as the subjective self, is not the historical Christ, but rather, the formless, mystical, eternal Christ, the Christ of grace, transformation, and the Eucharist. As the human manifestation of God, Christ is more subjective to us than the Holy Spirit, which has no human manifestation, and therefore remains as the objective stillpoint, or light at the center. Thus, despite their unity, Christ as the subjective vessel and the Spirit as its objective interior focal point are two different experiences of God.

If, on the basis of consciousness, Christ is too subjective to be known objectively, then, on the basis of intellect, Christ is unbelievable as our personal, subjective experience. Because our minds insist on retaining the image and idea of the historical Christ, we are kept from identifying him as our subjective, mystical, interior reality. More often than not, we only recognize Christ outside ourselves and, interiorly, do not know him at all. We often take him for the stillpoint, the center of being, the Holy Spirit; this is all right, since they are one, but it still falls short of God's purely *human* manifestation in ourselves. The failure to overcome this duality and realize this identity is a great stumbling block that keeps us from realizing in what way Christ is manifest in us, here and now, as our true self.

With this experience, I saw that Christ's primary message was the mature acceptance of our humanity, our selfhood—a unitive selfhood, and that it was only by accepting this that we could go beyond self to pure vision. As God, Christ's feat was just this: the full acceptance of his human manifestation, the living of his humanity completely, even unto death. In like fashion, the feat of the new man, the Christ-self, is equally to accept this human dimension and live it fully—even unto death—for it is through this passage that we come to the final vision. At the time, although I saw all this clearly, I could not see how it worked; I could not see how, by accepting the self, one could go beyond the self.

Some years later, of course, I realized the whole movement of the unitive self was toward self-extinction and dissolution. It seems that, to return to the Father, the self, or unitive center, must be relinquished so God may be all—beyond subject and object. This relinquishing was Christ's own experience on the Cross and thus, when our true self dies, it is Christ giving up his self all over again; it is Christ that descends into hell (the great void) and Christ that rises again. What man ordinarily thinks of as his "self" is totally incapable of such a feat. Only Christ can take us through this passage; only he can save us and return us safely to the Father. Thus the first movement is the transformation of self into Christ, and the second movement, Christ's return to the Godhead.

Naturally, I saw none of this ahead of time. It seems God reveals His plan gradually lest we hold back out of fear and ignorance. Nevertheless, what I learned from this particular experience was very great. It gave me the necessary insight to accept this selfhood fully and go forward, with no strings attached. I did not know where I was going or how it would end; that I moved with God was all that mattered.

As a milestone, the experience resulted in a clean break with past experiences; I felt as if one part of my life was over and I now had to make a new beginning. Initially there was a sense of loss; the world was empty, everything was a wasteland before me, and I was not sure if I should be anxious about this or not. Was this really a step forward or, possibly, a step backward?

As it turned out, the preparation precluded anxiety; instead, there arose a great determination to go forth to a life of selfless giving; this was my chance to "give," to repay God for His graces, and to equalize the imbalance of love. Thus I went forward to realize how this new subjectivity worked in the most ordinary circumstances of everyday life.

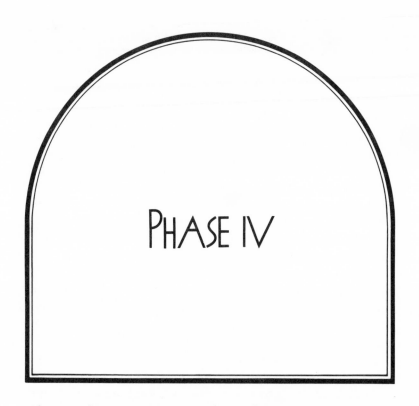

PHASE IV

This is where most contemplative literature comes to an end. It is assumed that after transforming union and spiritual marriage there is no further change or transformation and thus, there is nothing more to be said. After the glowing account of betrothal, marriage, and the honeymoon or post-marital experiences, no one says anything about the time after the honeymoon, when life settles down to the nitty-gritty of ordinary living. The failure to say anything about settling into a more mature stage leaves the false impression that the unitive life continues on in the same vein of transforming experiences, or is one continuous honeymoon.

What we have to admit is that any state, however ecstatic or delightful, cannot be maintained for any length of time without it growing commonplace and unspectacular. We have to face up to the fact that the transformation is over, the wedding and honeymoon are over, and we must now put these experiences behind and move courageously into a new life beyond transforming union. From now on, we look back on the transformation process as the child looks back on its embryonic period. Life in the chrysalis was very secure, the mechanism of transformation was a path in itself, but once the butterfly emerges, this secure path comes to an end, and the butterfly is virtually on its own. Thus it must fly into a new space, into the unknown—go forth to the full exercise of the mature unitive life.

The moment we step into this new dimension, we have already begun a life beyond transformation, a life which few people realize is actually a stage unto itself; a vital, crucial preparatory stage for yet a further change and transformation. Because no one realizes this, the stage has been given little coverage, has not been seen in its true perspective and, therefore, remains little understood. One reason is that to have perspective—on anything—we need distance; that is, we must have passed through a stage before we can look back and see it for what it is. This is the same principle as not seeing the forest for the trees: in order to see the forest we have to get beyond the trees. Because the butterfly can look back on the transforming process, he can tell us about it, but he cannot tell us about the complete butterfly stage because he is not yet beyond it. But once beyond, in a further state, he can look back on the mature unitive life and see it in its true perspective, can understand it in a way he could not while it was in progress.

The mature unitive stage is a recapitulation of Christ's active life, a life that led to his death, an unusual death in that it was more than his physical dissolution; rather, it was the type of death that led to the resurrection—the eternal vision beyond self. The mature unitive life, then, is the preparation for this death, the death of the Christ-self—the unitive self. However nondual and subjective the unitive center, it is still an object of consciousness in that we can reflect on our union with God—

just as Christ did. As stated elsewhere, death of the unitive self is the death of both God and self as reflective objects of consciousness, followed by the birth of God as pure subjectivity, God's own way of knowing all that exists—the Eye seeing Itself. It is this transition between God-as-object and God-as-subject that takes place between Cross and Resurrection.

For most authors, the contemplative life ends on the downbeat of the soul's plunging into the world of social welfare and reform, of missionary or charitable work. It is said that after his years in the sheltered cocoon, the individual now rejoins society to roll up his sleeves, get to work, and finally do something for God and man. What these authors do not realize is that the butterfly can never rejoin the caterpillars as long as he lives. The butterfly is not an extraordinary caterpillar; rather, he is a different type altogether.

When the butterfly returns, the caterpillars do not recognize him anymore: he is an outsider. Nobody wants what he has to give; nobody is interested in his new knowledge. If the butterfly tries to give them some perspective on their creeping lives they are outraged, call him a fraud, and bring him down. They may even put him to death. Because the butterfly has returned full and overflowing, being dismissed, ignored, and misunderstood is a bewildering predicament. Like Santa Claus returning with good things for all men, he discovers he cannot give anything away. What we have here is no success story; there will be no glory in this unitive life. It will not be easy—indeed, Christ lasted only three years among the caterpillars. Yet to be put down, put out, and put away is the way it is supposed to go. To be rejected is the way forward now; it is the essence of the new movement, and what will demand the exercise of the full unitive life.

The illusion to dispel, an illusion held by many contemplative authors, is that one who comes to this state is automatically known, recognized, accepted, revered, and eventually canonized. The opposite is true, of course; this was not the way it went for Christ. Looking back on Christ, our perspective has obliterated the reality of his immediate predicament. Apart from a few weak friends, he was not recognized or accepted and, if he had not been divine, we would never have heard from him again. It is important to remember that he was vindicated after his death, not before.

Since, in their own way, the caterpillars have love for God and neighbor, we may ask in what way the butterfly is different, or what there is about the transforming process that makes the difference. More than anything else, I think, the butterfly has an unusual freedom and independence; he is a "law unto himself." He is independent of people, things, status, institutions, and free from fear. He is not out to please, impress, or play roles, and if he gets the chance to be outspoken, others will rush to throw him out. Yet the butterfly is not a rebel, a revolutionary, or a reformer; he does not have to be—just his presence among the caterpillars is disturbing enough. In a word, he does not fit into this world's society and its ways of thinking. Not even remotely.

The goal of the butterfly is not to live for God or neighbor but rather, to live with God and with neighbor— with God being the joy; with neighbor being the problem. The soul moves forward with God to exercise its whole being by refusing nothing, running from nothing, taking the hurdles, and standing tall in the face of failures and trials, with an undauntable spirit that can never be brought low. It takes tremendous faith and insight to see that the way forward is the exercise of the mature adult life, and that the only goal is to be as fully as possible what God created us to be, to deal courageously with life as we find it. We have already learned there is nothing we can give God that He does not have already; nothing we can do for God that He cannot do better. What we can do, however, is live the unitive life to its fullest potential.

This may sound easy, but in reality, nothing is more difficult.

The mature unitive state is not an altruistic state or a life lived for others. What we love in others, the good we see in them, is God. Actually there is no union between people; their union can only come about through their union with God. Thus we can be one with each other only because we are one with God. Any other type of oneness—mind, body, feelings, etc.—is completely superficial. It is because our unity lies in God that we can love others with an unconditional love that is not dependent upon what they do, how they treat us, their personalities, and so on. Thus what we have here is not really love for others, but love of God *in* others. I regard this love as the essence of Christian charity, for there is no other way to "love our enemies"—the ultimate challenge of love Christ put to us.

Too often what goes by the name of love is nothing more than external works, or what we do for others. It is important to distinguish Christian love and works of human decency, which are incumbent upon all peoples of the earth, be they believers or unbelievers. The mandate to feed the hungry, for example, bypasses religion, race, or political persuasion; it is not particularly Christian.

Since the exercise of selfhood will be the primary activity of this state, it is important, then, to have a correct idea of what "active" means in the context of the unitive life. As already indicated, good works and love of neighbor are not the focal point or goal. Like everyone else, the contemplative is sensitive to the needs of others, but he does nothing to get something, does nothing for the sake of self-gratification. What he does for others he counts as of no great importance, since he knows that anything he can do is but temporary and superficial; it does not have any deep, lasting, spiritual effect. He cannot give grace, light, or interior vision; he cannot tap into the depths of another soul or bring about their transformation—he has no power of his own. Though his works derive from the unitive center—and therein lies their merit and worth—he cannot be God to others, and though he prays to be a medium of good, he cannot make it happen, and has no illusions in this matter. Perhaps the highest charity of all occurs when we have become so pure and perfect we become mediums of God's love in such a way that his love can pass through us without our knowing, or without knowingly having done a single thing.

Christ affirmed that he did not do his works through his own power, but through the power of the Father; thus his works were not his own. It might also be added that Christ was not involved in social work. As harsh as it may sound, his miracles had as their end that others might believe in his divine mission; their end was not solely to cure physical and social ills. Had this been his purpose, he could have cured everyone—remade the world, in fact—but this was not his mission or his message. In fact, he was rejected because he was not a cure-all for the ills of society; his kingdom was not of this world.

I see Christ first and foremost as a mystic who had the continuous vision of God and whose mission was to share it, give it to others. Few people see it this way; instead, they have exploited Christ's good works to justify their own busy lives, lives without interior vision and therefore lives without Christ. As already said, performance of our duties and responsibilities as human beings, respect for the rights of others, lending a helping hand, are what it means to be human; there is nothing particularly Christian about it.

The point to be made is that the butterfly is one who has his priorities right, and sees through the superficiality and often self-invested interests of the "active" life. His zeal for others is only that he be a medium of vision, a vision he realizes only God can give. That he is powerless to give the vision is his suffering. It is a terrible thing to live your whole life intensely with God and not be able to convey God to others; there is anguish in this that finds no relief in external works. In fact, the inability to find adequate expression for the interior vision is the type of suffering peculiar to this state, for nothing but sharing the vision is satisfying. And since nobody wants this vision, one must bear it alone, and therein lies the suffering.

Inadequate expression of the inner flame, its failure to be revealed or accepted, gives rise to the totally non-gratifying, selfless aspect of this stage. Though it is the mature stage of selfhood, it is not a stage for self-fulfillment in the sense of being personally satisfying, rewarding, or successful; rather, it is the stage of selfless fulfillment—in other words, to give all and to receive nothing. But then, what can this world give? Can it add to wholeness? Can it go deeper than the deepest dimension of existence? How to advance once we have come this far is a peculiar problem; it is like searching for a path through space. Yet the butterfly knows there has to be more and, in time, discovers another way forward.

The primary movement within this phase is coming upon, what I call, the "open mind," and because it is so important I have set it aside for special treatment in the next chapter. But apart from this open mind, the way forward in this stage is by way of suffering, trials, and tribulations of all kinds; these factors enable us to exercise the unitive life. Thus these particular problems are state-bound, and cannot be rightly understood in any other light, or known at any other stage.

Because he can fly high, the butterfly naturally has a different perspective, a different vision which, unfortunately, he cannot share with those who are still earth-bound. At first it is difficult for the butterfly to accept this fact, accept his own differences; he cannot understand what keeps him from sharing the inner flame, or why others are incapable of receiving it. This continually brings him back to the knowledge that of himself he can do nothing; all he can do is pray to be a medium of God's grace. It is the repeated recognition of his powerlessness to express the inner flame that finally brings him to see that this flame is not his own. He cannot pass it along or have it light the way for others; he cannot use it for his own ends, however good those ends may be. With this recognition, he begins to understand that this flame has another purpose altogether, which is to burn him out through his very inability to express it. It is as if the flame wears down the self through the self's continual search for the flame's adequate expression or manifestation— hence the life of unfulfilled giving. The self is not burned out through exhausting external works; rather, the self is burned out interiorly by the very inability to be exhausted. So the flame burns on, ever propelling us outward in the hope of someday finding its true and adequate expression—to set the world on fire, perhaps—while all the while, unknown to us, we are being burned out, and the unitive self is disappearing into the flame, being consumed by it.

If, let us say, the flame could reach to the outside to find its perfect outlet or expression, there would be no burning out or consummation on the inside, for once on the outside, the flame would dissipate itself and become lost to us. This is what would happen if, even for a time, we were allowed the great satisfaction of its full recognition. But this is not what the flame is about; its purpose is not to set the world on fire or to accomplish anything in our exterior lives. Rather, its sole purpose is to interiorly consume its unitive partner. As said before, this flame is an intense living, not a living *for* God, but a living *with* God. It is a totally subjective experience, the experience of the whole self living to the fullest extent of its potential which, somehow, is not enough.

Initially I regarded this flame as belonging equally to myself and God; therefore, it was a bewildering discovery to learn that it was not mine and never had been. But the day I saw this, I also realized that its expression would only have been self-expression, and that the resulting satisfaction would have accrued to the self and not to God. In this way I saw that self cannot truly express God by any efforts of its own; only God can express Himself. What this is saying is that the unitive self is not an adequate expression of God; it cannot, in fact, express Him at all. In turn, I am convinced that this is why it was necessary for Christ to give up his unitive self on the cross—because it was only this way, without a self, that he could become the adequate expression of God. Without the self, he could effect in us what he could not effect as long as self remained.

Once fully entrenched in this stage, I began to see the unfolding of some mysterious plan of God in this deep burning out of self, and saw that what I should really be doing—instead of running around looking for the flame's outward expression—was to sit still and allow the flame to consume me in short order—quickly, that is. The trouble is, I could not do it. Another day and I would see an opening—a chance to express the flame—and say to myself: "This is it!" Then I would rush in where angels fear to tread. Naturally it all came to naught; every plan, every work, every effort exploded in my face, and I was burned outside as well as inside.

Another intuition was that things could not go on this way forever; sooner or later something had to give. If not destined to die soon, I could not keep running with this flame forever. Sometimes I thought of myself as an Olympic runner, always running to pass the torch to the next runner; only no one appeared and I had to keep running. Once it occurred to me that from the beginning of man's time, God has always had His torch runners, running through every generation so that man's love for God would never go out until the last man on earth died.

I finally decided that, since the flame had no way to the outside, it would simply have to explode someday. I had no idea what would happen then, but was sure it would be something wonderful—the ultimate of all possible expressions! Eventually this explosion did occur, but it was nothing like I expected—it was just a puff! A silent puff and the flame went out. With this, however, the entire unitive center disappeared, and what remained was absolute stillness and silence. There was no movement at all, and also no sense of emptiness, because now there was no longer a "within" and therefore nothing left to be empty. What happens after this, however, is another story.

What I would stress is that the unitive stage is not truly a stage for expressing the fruits of transformation—as many tend to believe. Though the self will be fully exercised and there is much activity, this activity is relatively superficial and comes to naught. I do not see this as a self-fulfilling stage or one of interior satisfaction; rather, it is a stage of God-fulfillment in that, unknown to us—and even against the self—God is consuming the self.

I cannot help but think it was the same burning movement of the interior flame that informed Christ of his impending death. Somehow he saw the nature of his final consummation as one that would be far more than his physical death. He saw this as the only way to be the true medium of God: to accomplish after death what he could not accomplish by his works in this life. I believe he, too, saw the unfolding of a great plan, and knew that in the return to the Father he would have to go beyond his self—his divine, unitive self. Christ's death was indeed an explosion—one that will echo for all time. It was his explosion into the Godhead, into the full subjectivity of God.

It seems Christ's earthly problem is akin to our own problem in the unitive state, which is that of lighting the spark in others, handing on the flame, lighting up the world. Since the flame cannot be generated from the outside, he had to find a way to generate it from within. That the Holy Spirit came as a flame, a light within, is the way it worked, for it is only in this light that we can know the subjectivity of Christ. As long as his human self remained, it would always be an object to us—in the same way all selves are objects. Thus he had to relinquish that self in order to reveal his subjectivity, his oneness with us. And it is the Spirit that lights up this subjectivity, reveals it to us, and enables us to understand it. Thus the Spirit is Christ's gift to us and Christ is the Spirit's gift to us. Every way we look at it, it is all God's gift of Himself to man, pressed down on us and overflowing. Indeed, everywhere we turn, everywhere we look, God is revealing Himself.

In some small way the exercise of the unitive stage follows the same pattern as Christ's active life, follows it even to the death of the self on the cross. We have accepted our selfhood, our humanity, and spent our lives doing all we could to express its inner depths and share the vision with others. Like Christ we have been rejected and not understood; we have had to go it alone. In the meantime, we are consumed by the interior flame, and dying in a way we may never fully understand. The purpose of this stage, then, is to bring us to the cross, and there to give up and go beyond the unified self.

As I see it, those who deny their selfhood and their humanity thereby fail to recognize it as the passageway through which all men must pass. They fail not only to be what they were created to be, but fail to meet their true destiny, which lies beyond selfhood. To go beyond the self there must first be a self, a whole self—a Christ self. Caterpillars die everyday; some never make it through the cocoon, some die as soon as they emerge. But others live through the mature stage of the butterfly and exercise it as fully as was meant to be. And once exercised—to a fullness only God knows—the butterfly dies and thereby comes to the eternal vision.

If there is another way to go beyond the self without passing through it, I do not know what that would be. It seems logical that we would have to go through the self to get to the other side or beyond it; otherwise, by circumventing the obvious, we fool ourselves by denying its existence. I am convinced that the passage through selfhood is the particular "way" Christ pointed out, and that pointing out this way of salvation was his particular message and mission. That others see Christ's mission differently, I do not deny. Without height, the caterpillars have a limited perspective and therefore a limited interpretation of Christ's mission. And if there is anything troublesome about the caterpillars' interpretation it is that they continually impose their limited perspective on the rest of us. This is untenable.

Strictly speaking, the problem with the interior flame cannot be called "suffering"; it is more of a bewildering predicament, but one I regard as the most consistent and prominent feature of the unitive stage. There is, however, a type of deep suffering that can be encountered here, a type I call by its experiential reality "a broken heart." This is how it comes about.

As we all know, there are a number of levels of personal satisfaction. We have just spoken of the lack of satisfaction with regard to expressing the inner flame, or bringing it to the outside. Another dissatisfying situation exists in the relationship between the butterfly and the caterpillar, because there can be no even exchange between them. Neither wants what the other has and, therefore, sharing is limited to a superficial, non-gratifying level. Put this together with the fact that, due to a different level of seeing and knowing, the butterfly's insights are not understood or valued, and we can see why the butterfly is a destined loner. Because there is no personal gratification on a purely human level, this is a very solitary state, and over a period of time this solitude can become a difficult cross to bear. Though never without deep joy at the center, at the level of the human heart there is indeed a deficit of joy, a deficit that becomes so weighty it eventually breaks the heart in two. When this happens, we are in a position to identify with the woman whose heart was "pierced with a sword," in a position to understand it experientially.

The pierced heart is not any single thing; rather, it is a combination of the inability to share what matters most in our life, the rejection of the best in ourselves, the continuous giving without receiving, a sensitive and loyal heart that has been taken for granted, stepped on, denied, betrayed—pierced. It is a heart that has to keep so much to itself or within itself, that it breaks from the sheer weight of this burden. In a word, it is a heart that can find no true or lasting satisfaction in this world and thus longs for the vision with ever growing intensity. But the marvel of this heart is that the heavier the burden, the clearer the vision, and so true did I find this, I can say: a broken heart is the pathway to vision.

There is no problem here with lack of conformity to God's will, no breakdown of union, or pain at the center; this is no dark night. Yet the dying human heart is a deep wound to the self, a death blow that reaches into the roots of human existence. We hear about the suffering heart of Christ and his mother, and do not realize it is the reality of a dying self; a tragedy by human standards, yet a divine undoing, a call to surrender the human heart to God. Thus the affective joy of deep, lasting human companionship has been cut off, and all that remains is the joy at the center, wherein God is everything to us that people and this world are not. This further death of self is the very heart of the unitive life and its true purpose. It is the result of living alone with God, of being a butterfly with a different way of seeing and knowing; in a word, the butterfly lives in a different landscape altogether. But this is the price to be paid for union with God, a price that costs dearly in all areas of our humanity and selfhood.

One day I had a particular insight into this broken heart. It happened when I was seriously considering getting rid of it—unloading the whole burden, changing my life style and going in search of a more gratifying existence. I knew that with the broken heart some part of me was dying, and I thought it might only be leading to some psychologically sick condition; after all, how much human gratification can man live without? At what point does it verge on the psychologically unsound? How much deprivation can we take—or should we take? Poised on the moment of decision, I put it all to God, and in that instant came upon a bewildering, if not frightening reality. I saw I was indeed dying to all sense of personal existence, but at the same time the inner flame rose up—it reminded me of the angel's flaming sword guarding the door to paradise—and seemed to forbid any fear to enter. Within this great flame was a small, flickering, helpless flame—my self—and I could see it was about to be extinguished—hence the fear. But the greater flame which prohibited any fear to enter indicated one thing to me: let the self die, let it go, do nothing about it, let everything be as it is. I knew then the dying self was all in God's mysterious plan; it was His will, and because it was His will all things would be well. So I went on carrying this heavy heart around, knowing that the cross God had given only He could take away. Though I could keep running and protesting all my life, it would not do the least bit of good. Our tryst was the cross, and the trysting place was the human heart.

Since I had never heard of a further loss of self, I was in the dark as to the true meaning of all this. But I knew all that was necessary to know—namely, that God was in charge; it was His doing. I had simply to let Him have His way, do His work without fear, and had to trust Him with my very life—my self. Never did I see this as a preparation for a great journey, a crossing over into a new life and a new state of consciousness. I never realized that the continuous vision behind the door at the center was daily becoming more imminent.

Actually, I never believed in the destruction of the self, the unified self; and even toward the end of this phase I wrote, "For me, destruction of the self is an impossible fear. I do not believe the self is capable of being destroyed." The context was that any disintegration would only result in re-integration, for even if we went to pieces and stayed that way for the rest of our lives, these pieces would not disappear—what would be left if they did? In this matter I often referred back to an experience I had when I was fifteen and, unknowingly, was still in a state of pieces or disunity. For a time, God held me in such a tight unity that I thought to myself: If He puts me down now, releases His hold, or moves away, I will go to pieces. I could see myself going back to the usual searching, distracted mind, the dissatisfied will, the restless state—in a word, the whole war of nature and grace. After knowing such a powerful unity, going back to such a fractured state was almost frightening. As it turned out, God let me down so gradually and gently I was amazed how He could do this without my having any experience of going to pieces. It seems that, along with the experience, we are given a fortifying, strengthening grace, and I am convinced that it is the buildup or accumulation of this imperceptible grace that gradually brings about a permanent state of unity. Because this takes place on an imperceptible level—a mystical level of grace, as I see it—once the state becomes permanent we often fail to realize just how powerful and tight this unity really is. Thus it is good sometimes to feel ourselves on the verge of dissolution so that, by sheer contrast, we may know the unity in which God holds us and understands that, without His grace, we would be back where we started—in pieces.

For this reason I always held that disunity or disintegration could only lead back to unity; this was the only way it could go. I might add that, even with the final loss of self, this unity is not "undone"; there is no going to pieces; this is not the way it happens. Instead, the self, the entire center, enters God in one piece because pieces of self cannot enter into the unity of God; rather, it is the whole self that dissolves into the wholeness of God. Consequently, a premature attempt to forego the self in piecemeal fashion, or before we have it all together, is destined to failure. I do not see it happening. Like the all-or-none law, we go completely, wholly, or we do not go at all.

For much of this unitive phase I kept journals, and from these it is evident that, because of the obvious indestructibility of the unitive center, I looked upon selfhood as akin to Godhood. Though everything in the world is taken from us, the center lives on, remains untouched; what is more, I was amazed that the center did not wear out from all the buffeting, testing, and pounding it had to take. My conclusion was that it was certainly God's sanctuary, an impregnable fortress that could withstand every contrary force in this world; indeed, the gates of hell could not prevail against it! The idea that this selfhood, this Godhood, could be destroyed, that it could eventually disappear, was totally unthinkable.

As said before, the unitive center was both an object of vision and an automatic awareness—like a feeling or sixth sense, which we do not have to see to know. What obscured the full vision of God at the center was the true self lying over it as a door or veil. Though I had but few glimpses of the true self—the Christ-self—at the center, I always thought of it as part and parcel of the central strength, the inner fortress, the living flame; thus self as part of God was indestructible, and I never gave a thought as to how it would be left behind when coming into the permanent vision in the next life. I gave no thought as to "what" would behold this vision. For some reason this question never entered my mind; yet I see now this is the greatest, most important question a being can ask.

As it stood, in my entire life I never spent more than a half hour thinking about the self. As a separate subject it did not interest me, and as a subjective reality I never had to think about it. From earliest childhood I regarded the self as the totality of my being, and that was basically the end of the subject. Because of this background it was an ironic destiny to experience the dissolution of self, and that I came upon some hard times in the journey may well be due to this lack of expectation, or to a deficit in my background of knowledge. Yet this fact made me all the more dependent upon God for help and insight and, in the long run, may have worked to my advantage. But one thing I know: if the falling away of the unitive self had been an ordinary expectation or a casual happening, I would not be writing now or have written my earlier account. The complete surprise, the bewilderment, the extraordinary aspect of it was such that, for the rest of my life, there may be nothing more important to talk about. The point, however, is not to warn other contemplatives, nor even to debate the subject—which, after all, is a foregone conclusion—but to have them include it with their ordinary expectations, to incorporate it within their present system of mystical theology, to study its prospects and, above all, to be prepared for such a happening.

So far we have gone over two ways in which the soul can suffer in this stage: it suffers because it cannot share the inner flame or find its adequate outward expression, and it suffers from a lack of personal self-gratification, which is a deep loneliness that only the eternal vision can fill. Other hardships to be endured are the trials and tribulations common to every man, and if mine were any different, it was due to their sheer number and variety. A compendium of these trials might look like a modern-day list of St. Paul's casualties: robbed three times, carwrecked once, fired many times, and so on. Though I was never stoned, I would substitute for this the fact that I was once egged; yes, indeed, egged by my beloved students. But the ignominy of these trials is that I could not claim that they were endured for any great cause. Though

I may have lived my life as intensely with God as did St. Paul, there was no satisfaction in the knowledge that my sufferings counted for a thing; in fact, I saw them as a waste because they accomplished nothing, were getting me nowhere, and certainly were no good to anyone else.

If there was any immediate value in these trials it was that they eventually became commonplace and, therefore, unchallenging, which kept me on the lookout for variety and change. When one is used to clearing twenty-foot hurdles every day, it becomes routine, and there enters the search for some new level of existence that can be tapped into or tested.

If there was a single trouble I did not encounter, it was deep within the interior center. Only at this depth did I feel I truly lived, for outside this center I viewed life as relatively superficial, humorous—a "stage," as Shakespeare put it. I could not possibly have become attached to it, though I sometimes made concerted efforts to do so. From sheer continuity and repetition, trials and tribulations eventually became like water rolling off a duck's back, and when this happened I felt I had come to some mysterious ending. It is at this point that the self has obviously outworn its usage, and when there is nothing left to challenge the self, we are ready to move into a new dimension of living, that of a life without a self.

Before we can make this move, however, the ability to take all the hurdles in routine fashion must have become an ingrained habit of soul, an unconscious way of life, because even though the self disappears, the trials and tribulations of life go right on. We can still be thrown to the lions, but with no self, from what comes the courage, the inner determination, the psychological stamina? It is an illusion to think that without a self the world suddenly changes and all our problems and sufferings come to an end; on the contrary, they may become worse than ever! The question is: what endures these trials, what survives them, what lives on in this totally helpless state? Discovering the answer to these questions only comes through living in this state, and anything that can be said about it beforehand is difficult to believe—and even harder to convey.

All we need to know is that we meet obstacles and hurdles in the same way when there is no self, as when we have a self, which means the conditioning has become such an unconscious habit that we would not know how to live or behave otherwise. Few people realize what it takes to live without a self. The preparation has to be tough and thorough; the inner center must first have proven itself impregnable and immovable under fire and stress. Otherwise God cannot entrust us to the powerful waters that will carry us into another dimension of life. Thus one sign that the unitive stage is coming to an end is the eventual failure of anything—even the greatest of trials—to challenge the unified self anymore. This indicates we have come a long way, run our course to the finish, and come through with such an unshakable trust in God that we are beyond the very need for trust. Life with God is so taken for granted, such a totality of our lives that the very need to think of Him is a lack of trust itself.

All this illustrates that loss of self takes place on a totally mundane level of practical, everyday living. It does not come about by some great insight or enlightenment— which is transient at best—it is not lost through some psychologically traumatic event, or lost in a state of ecstasy. The self is not merely "seen through," it is *lived* through—lived to its dire end. Once we come to this end there will occur moments of realizing its absence, and there will be a period of acclimating to this absence, acclimating to the irreversible closedown of a self-conscious system. But all this is after the fact, and has nothing to do with the daily consummation of the self.

The essence of the unitive life, then, is the gradual imperceptible death of the self, a death made possible because the self is secured, anchored in God so that it has no fear of living fully, accepting all the suffering, heart-aches, and trials that come its way. The mechanism of the self's dying is built into its life with God—we give all, He takes all, and when all is gone, He alone remains. Without this unitive life we cannot possibly give up the self; there would not be sufficient security, love, trust, or even a sufficient reason to do so.

Thus far we have been considering the trials and tribulations of the unitive life, and have said nothing as yet of selfless giving, which has a definition and challenge of its own. I regard selfless giving as behavior governed by what is right and best in every situation and relationship, as opposed to behavior that is governed by how we feel—our emotions and sentiments. To give of ourselves does not mean we are yes-men, or that we give in for the sake of peace, personal satisfaction, or to gain the approval of others. In certain circumstances, the best thing we may be able to do for our neighbor is to do nothing, for example—not allowing others to depend on us to their own detriment. When we permit others to lean on us for their psychological well-being, we rob them of their independence and freedom, de-energize them as leeches do their victims. What sometimes passes for love and charity, or even therapy, is a subtle mask for this type of psychological vampirism, otherwise known as transference, or the guru syndrome. The baby bird does not know he can fly until his mother pushes him from the nest; the zen student does not know he can see until the master slams the door in his face. This kind of charity sounds callous, but, in fact, it is a matter of wisdom, a matter of right timing and, above all, a selfless caring for the good of others. There will be times, of course, when for the good of others we must be long-suffering, patient, remain silent, or put up with trying circumstances; but we do it not from emotional involvement or because there is no other way out, but from a higher level of insight, wherein there is no concern for personal gain. Selfless giving, then, means putting a higher principle and the good of others before anything else. It does not mean putting others before our self; this is not the choice involved. The deeper self is too well taken care of to be a consideration; there is no need to make a choice between me or you.

One way or the other, selfless giving and all trials of the unitive life are a test of virtue, a practice of it. At one point it occurred to me that there may be no such thing as multiple virtues, because in the strength of the center all virtues appear as one. St. John of the Cross affirms this when he says that a "single hair" of strength holds them in unity, so there is but one virtue and one strength.

Each of us, however, will have a label for that virtue which best epitomizes all the rest, a virtue we desire most to master or in which we feel deficient. For myself, I felt patience was the summation of all I needed to master in this area, for if one could be truly patient, there could never be a movement toward blame, judgment, or a sharp tongue. Instead, there would be perfect detachment and charity; in a word—there would be no interior movement at all. On one occasion I came upon an interesting discovery regarding the true nature of patience.

I had been listening to a three-year-old having a tantrum—screaming, carrying on something awful; it probably lasted fifteen minutes. Ordinarily, I would have walked away from such behavior or turned up the music, but this day I decided to sit quietly and watch my interior reactions, without doing a thing. First I noticed that there was no emotional movement within, and that the screaming had robbed me of all thought; I was, in fact, in a silent, motionless state. But then I had a vision: I saw every tiny nerve in my body become unhinged, like a chain of links quietly coming undone—dissolving. Then it occurred to me that patience, and perhaps all virtue, had a great deal to do with our nerves, and that the essence of virtue was to be completely unnerved—to have no nerves at all, that is. What could possibly try us if we had no nerves? Such a bodiless condition would be near to a heavenly state; indeed, one could walk through fire, through death itself, unscathed and untouched. I thought this would be ideal, and afterwards paid more attention to my nervous system in the practice of virtue, for I was now sure there was a link between them. I might add that the strength at the center makes it possible to observe the nervous system because the center is non-emotional anyway. This watching entails a certain body awareness and is, I think, a great help in the practice of virtue. We may have no desire or inclination to hurt others, but how often must we do battle with our nervous system in order to reflect this good will? Anyway, I felt this was a positive practice, and the day I could sit in the midst of absolute chaos with a perfectly still nervous system, I felt I had come a long way.

Unfortunately, the world has no value for such mastery. In a school where I taught it was a standing joke that whenever I lectured, anybody and everybody could crawl in and out the windows without my noticing a thing—as if I were blind or something! I regarded these antics as attention-getting behaviors and decided if I ignored them they would eventually wear themselves out—which proved to be true. But if I had the patience to win out, the administration did not. In the long run, I was fired for allowing this monkey business, and in leaving could not refrain from suggesting that instead of a teacher they hire a zookeeper.

But what, we might ask, does this have to do with selfless giving? As I saw it, patience—or any virtue we wish to practice—is not only a death blow to the self, which otherwise would vent itself, or reach out to shake others up, but it is the death blow to the nervous system, which eventually must conform to the knowledge of what is right, best, and wisest in human nature. There are no rewards for this type of selflessness. Others certainly do not appreciate it, and there is no reward in doing what is right when it is the only thing we can do. Thus there comes the point where acting any other way is unnatural, a point where good habits cannot be reversed, and a point of no return to the self. From here on we have no choice but to move steadily forward into a selfless state.

Though hundreds of examples could be given regarding the practice and testing of virtue or selfless giving, this is not to our purpose. All we have wanted to do is give some idea of how the unitive state is exercised; how, through every test, challenge, trial, and suffering, the soul is being prepared and toughened as it moves forward to encounter another transformation—a radical change of consciousness—that results when the unitive life comes to an end, or when the self falls away and God becomes all.

The perfect note on which to end this chapter would be to turn to St. John of the Cross to see what he has to say of this stage, but, alas, if we do so, we will only find he has nothing to say. He is still back in the honeymoon stage recounting its transient experiences, which, while they are real glimpses beyond the self, do not tell us how to get there or how, in this life, the mysterious workings of the inner flame bring this about. Like myself, he seems not to have questioned "what" it is that sees the vision once the self is left behind in death. He never seems to doubt, however, that it will be left behind, and one of his poems reflects this ardent desire for the self's demise.

I no longer live within myself
And I cannot live without God
For if I have neither Him nor myself
What will life be?

It will be a thousand deaths,
Longing for my true life
*And dying because I do not die.**

It would be difficult to find a more adequate expression of the desire for the final death of the self and the unveiled vision of God. When he says "I die because I do not die," he puts his finger on the very mechanism of the self's dying—the living flame consuming without exhausting. It is like saying: I die because I live—die to myself because I live with God. And to live with God means He consumes all we have to give until there is nothing left; thus in its very giving the self dies. While we can rest assured that St. John of the Cross came into the full vision of his quest, he unfortunately left no account of how it finally came about, nor left any map of how we might find our way to the same end.

St. Teresa, on the other hand, while she does not take us beyond this full unitive stage, nevertheless regards it as the seventh and highest mansion of the interior life. Once spiritual marriage has been attained, she tells us the effects of this state. First and foremost, there is the continuous passive awareness of God within; there is the coming together of Martha and Mary in the indistinguishable living of the active and contemplative life; it is a state notable for "forgetfulness of self; a desire to suffer; deep interior joy in persecution; a desire to serve; great detachment; and no fear of the devil's deceits."**Also noteworthy is that the seventh mansion is relatively unspectacular compared to the two preceding mansions; there is a settling down to a deeper dimension of living,

---

*"Stanzas of the soul that suffers with longing to see God," *Collected Works,* trans. Kavanaugh and Rodriguez.
**Saint Teresa de Avila, *Collected Works,* translated by Kieran Kavanaugh and Otilio Rodriguez (Washington: Institute of Carmelite Studies, 1976).

and a cessation of the former ecstatic states and experiences. In other words, the marvels of transformation are over, the goal has been accomplished and, as we know from her later life and travels, St. Teresa gave full vent to the exercise of the unitive state. If I have any criticism, it is with her lack of the foresight that would provide for the full exercise of the seventh mansion, for those in her "dovecotes" of prayer. It did not occur to her that the exercise of the unitive life is state-bound—not just a matter of having a special apostolic mission. Not everyone can be a foundress, but the interior energy that propels such an endeavor, that accepts and desires all such challenges, is the same for all.

To the question of why St. Teresa and other saints did not come upon a further transformation, or a more radical change of consciousness, we can only answer that it was not the will of God. There is no reason to suspect that, on their part, the saints were lacking in fortitude, generosity, or the psychological stamina necessary for this further movement. They held back nothing from God, and would have given their all had they been asked to do so. Thus, as to why they were not asked to do so, there is no answer, but that a further movement was an imminent possibility, is a sure fact. Of the numerous descriptions given by the mystics regarding their upper-division experiences, I have chosen the following to illustrate this possibility.

During this state of spiritual death the enraptured soul loses all sense of its own being, but on regaining consciousness it is cognizant of its own separate existence as a creature and of God's threefold nature . . . Consider one more point: during the highest form of rapture, a ray of refining light emitted by the Godhead, darts toward the soul and purifies it. Blinded by this incomprehensible light, the soul becomes oblivious of itself and its own individuality, physically languid, spiritually inactive, and exanimated. Nor are we to wonder

at this because the enraptured soul, lost to its own
*being and found in the Supreme Being . . .**

From this description it is obvious that a state exists
beyond union where no duality between God and self is
experienced; duality only reappears when the mystic falls
back into ordinary consciousness. This tells us that consciousness is responsible for man's experience of duality,
and that such a consciousness has no place in eternal life.
The ultimate reality, then, knows no distinction between
itself and "other," because the other has been "exanimated"—become lifeless, selfless. Here there is no question of identity between the soul and God; rather, the soul
has died, undergone "spiritual death," and without a soul,
God is all that remains.

As long as the mystic continues to fall back into ordinary consciousness, his upper-division experiences are
only passing or transient. But should the time come when
he does *not* fall back into ordinary consciousness, then
he will have passed over the line to a new type of existence; he will have come upon a permanent state of no-
self.

The experience described by Suso is typical of experiences encountered during the third phase of unitive life,
which is a midpoint in our journey. For myself, this type
of experience was the turning point that enabled me to
put aside my life of experiences, because now I saw how
all my previous experiences had been tinged with self,
and having seen the real thing, it became impossible to
settle for less.

It is only after this third phase, or after many years
spent in a life of selfless giving, that this same experience
of "spiritual death" will once more present itself; only

---

*Henry Suso, *The exemplar: life and writings of Blessed Henry
Suso.* Ed. Nicholas Heller, trans. Ann Edward (Dubuque, Iowa: Priory
Press, 1962).

this time it will present the imminent possibility of becoming a permanent state. That is, the soul will never again fall back into ordinary consciousness. It is this imminent possibility that marks the final phase of the unitive life, and best defines the last stage of the journey. Later, I will have more to say about this, but for now, I would like to return to Suso's description.

When we read of this type of mystical experience, we tend to imagine the mystic lying on the floor completely unconscious—in his own words, he feels "lifeless." But the truth is that he is very much awake. For the first time in his life, perhaps, he is wide awake. The report of lifelessness, of being "exanimated" refers only to the death of a personal, individual life; for, after all, the mystic is very much alive—indeed, his "true life" remains. The fact that withdrawal of personal life immobilizes him completely only attests to his lack of preparedness; it attests to the fact there is too much self remaining, and that he has yet a long way to go. In other words, the disparity between his ordinary state and the new state of no-self is still too great to warrant its becoming a permanent reality. Thus it will take a more complete emptying of self before he is prepared to pass over the line of no-return. The fourth and fifth stages of the unitive life are this preparation. They intervene between the third stage and the final stage, and account for the difference between the experience of no-self being merely transitory and its becoming permanent. To my knowledge, this interval has never been accounted for in contemplative literature. And until it is accounted for, and understood, there will never be acceptance of a permanent state of no-self as a reality.

But this, at least, helps us to understand why, in the third phase of the journey, the mystic could not conceive of his enraptured state becoming a permanent reality in this life. Obviously he was not ready for it. Nevertheless, the mystics questioned or pondered whether or not such an experience could become permanent in the here and now. When the question was put to St. Bernard, he said, "I am not sure. Let those who have experienced it, come forward, for, as far as I can see, it is impossible."*

After relaying this anecdote, Suso, however, moves on to say that no-self, or the totally "self-abandoned man" can indeed become a permanent reality in this life. But the response of other authors to this inquiry gives the impression that the man who "comes forward" will instantly be pelted with rotten tomatoes—maybe even crucified. Why? Because, unwittingly, he is saying he is a man without sin! Needless to say, a man without a self is not about to stand up and say, "I have no sin." He cannot say this because the truth of the matter is: he has no "I." When there is no "who" anymore, the question of who sins or does not sin is a contradiction. The question cannot rightly be asked; it is not even relevant. Nevertheless, people will go on asking this question because they cannot separate physical presence from a self, or a self from sin. What they know in themselves is what they see in others, and there lies the unbridgeable gap, a terrible gap in understanding that will persist so long as self remains.

At any rate, we are getting closer to understanding why those who have come upon a permanent state of no-self are never heard from. Either they remain silent, or they will *be* silenced. Simple as that.

But even when a permanent state beyond union is denied, we still have to deal with those who regard this type of transient experience as potentially "dangerous." It is considered dangerous because the experience is saying that, in the next life, man has no consciousness of himself or of any separation from God. He loses his faculties and powers of soul; in a word, all that he knows about himself is not eternal. It is tantamount to saying

---

*Suso, *The Exemplar.*

that the individual soul is not eternal—depending, of course, on how "soul" is defined.

For some people, this lack of any feeling or knowledge of a personal "I" is a frightening prospect; frightening because it means they have yet a long way to go, and that there is no short cut to Christ's death and resurrection. The reality of no-self, however, can only be frightening to a watered-down Christianity, to an easy path of faith, and to a contemplative path that has mistaken the midpoint for the final goal. Yes, indeed, the permanency of an "exanimated" soul is an experience to be reckoned with!

That some of the well-known mystics did not leave us an account of this state is not proof that it was not known to others, nor proof that it, somehow, falls outside the tradition. No-self is actually a further step in the tradition, and if we do not find it up front, it is because it has been swept under the carpet; it has never been adequately understood.

The irony of the present-day situation is that with the East coming West, Christians are flooding Eastern markets, believing them privy to a mystical, contemplative dimension unknown to Christianity. Little do they realize what is waiting when the Eastern mystique wears off and the more proficient begin to emerge from their ranks. The very roots of Christianity are mystical, and the experiential reality of its truths have been passing quietly underground from one generation to another, lying in wait like a sleeping giant, poised to awaken in a less oppressive era. Underground through these dark ages of the Church, the contemplative community and its unknown mystics have been uninterruptedly nourished at the wellsprings of Christian mysticism. They have kept burning the light of the fullness of Christ's revelation, which goes beyond anything yet known to the East—unknown even to most Christians—a light that one day will encompass us all.

The revelation to the Hindu was the realization of his subjective oneness with God—his true self. This, too, was Christ's first message to us all, because it is the starting point of the good life, without which no man can follow him any further. But in the exercise of this unitive life, we go forward with Christ to his death on the cross, the surrender of the true self, and the only movement that can take us to the resurrection. Death of self is two things: it is the passing away or going beyond the sense of both the personal self and its unitive partner, or personal God. And what passes away is not only God and self as objects of consciousness,* but, surprisingly, the sense of self as subject of consciousness. The glory of the resurrection was Christ's realization of God as pure subjectivity, and his identity as all that is manifest of the Father.

As I see it, the movement beyond self, such as Christ knew on the cross and before the resurrection, is the further revelation given to the Buddhists. It is the close-down of a self-conscious mechanism, whereby the unitive center disappears, because it is the center of consciousness, and the medium of experiencing God to this point in time. This annihilation of self-consciousness goes beyond all notion and feeling of oneness, unity, and nonduality; it goes beyond all sense of a personal subject or self. But here the Eastern revelation comes to an end. It has been said that Buddha remained silent regarding the state beyond self; he had not a word to describe its reality; he had no light on it; there was nothing known to which he might compare it. Christ, however, broke this silence to become the light in the void, and to reveal to us yet

---

*As I have written elsewhere, despite his subjective (nondual) awareness of oneness with the Father, Christ always referred to him as other or as object to himself. He said repeatedly he did nothing of himself because power was given him by the Father; it was the Father who sent him and whose will he did. Continually, Christ prayed to the Father: in a word, the Father was an object to Christ's consciousness.

another dimension of existence, the resurrection and its particular type of "seeing"—the same whereby God sees Himself.

In this way, Christ incorporates the revelations of the East without invalidating them. He reconciles their two great traditions, adds to them, completes them, and unites them with himself in one final revelation of Truth. In so doing he corrects, as it were, or shortcuts the path to this final revelation by showing us that the "way" is not through rejecting our humanity or self-conscious state (which, after all, separates man from beast), but by accepting it as he did, and by realizing its fullest potential.

For some people, God's revelation to the East comes as news, but for the Christian contemplative there is nothing really new here. From the beginning, the notion of the Self as the unitive center has been well understood and realized in the ranks. The Buddhist finding of no-self, however, while it has obviously been experienced, has not been well defined in the Christian tradition, because it has not been sufficiently understood. But despite the breakdown of understanding, the truth of complete loss of self will continue to surface because it is inherent in the contemplative movement, and is the great reality for those destined to go all the way with Christ.

But there is another reason why the state beyond self has been de-emphasized and little known. After his resurrection, Christ was still in the flesh and, had it been beneficial to his mission, he could have remained on earth another fifty years. But as noted before, it was imperative to withdraw his objective presence in order that we realize his subjectivity in ourselves. In this way we can live his life again, die with him again, and be resurrected with him. Indeed, this is the nature of his continual subjective presence in the world, and his true oneness.

Christ's early ascension correctly de-emphasizes life on earth after the resurrection, because worldly life and society are not meant for the resurrected state. To get through this social jungle, man needs a unitive self—and one in top shape. It was this unitive self that Christ wanted for us first of all, because in the very exercise of this selfhood lies the mechanism of its death and transcendence. The great plan was to bring everyone to the unitive state because, once we get this far, Christ takes over; "what" goes beyond the self is obviously not the self; rather, it is Christ's subjectivity that remains when the self falls away. Thus, when the self dies or disappears it is Christ's journey all over again; it is the same vision and the same resurrection.

This means that the resurrected state has no place in this world, and that as man's last state on earth, many come to it in their final years and pass on immediately— much as Christ did. To live on, there is but one purpose, namely, to verify the resurrection as the true and final end of the unitive life—just as it was the verification of Christ's unitive life on earth. At the same time, it verifies and duplicates in lesser form Christ's own experience, and helps bring to light the true nature of his death, while allowing us to participate in the tremendous realization that took place at the resurrection. Apart from this, the state beyond self has no other place, purpose, or meaning in this world. Indeed, in claiming to have gone this far with Christ, one had better be well insulated against the barrage of objections and condemnations that are bound to come his way—in a word, he had better have nothing more to lose in this world.

That the saints and mystics held up as models of the unitive life were spared this condemnation, was undoubtedly God's plan for them. Their mission was to re-emphasize Christ's message of the true value and greatness of the unitive life, and once this mission was completed, they were not heard from again. This does not mean they went no further. It only means they were to say no more, and with this silence I find no objection.

To summarize the active phase this far, we can say it is noteworthy for the discovery that there is no true outlet or expression for the interior flame or unitive center. It seems man has outlets for all his other energies of mind, emotions, creativity, the body, and so on, yet no adequate expression for the type of energy we encounter at the center. Much of the suffering of this phase is due to this failure or inability. In time, however, we discover that we were only trying to express what was never ours from the beginning and that any expression would have been imperfect due to its admixture with the self. Thus we discover that we can only be pure mediums of God when there is no self remaining. This phase, then, is the time when God is burning out and consuming the self in a way we never thought possible; in truth, it is an imperceptible dying of the unitive self.

But there is yet another way the self is being put aside; this comes about with the discovery of a new movement, which I call "the open mind." Though not a separate phase in itself, I have nevertheless given it special coverage in the following chapter. Thus we turn now to say something of this new movement.

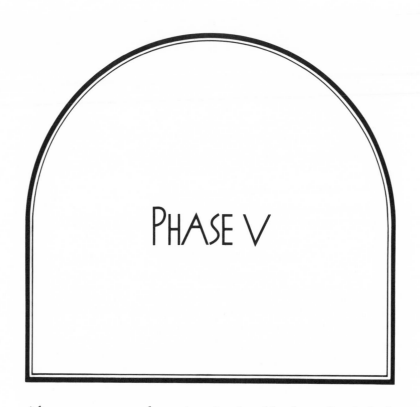

Phase V

After two years at the university, I suddenly realized I had not learned a thing. Despite the influx of information, nothing had really happened, I was the same person with the same mind—I had not grown at all. If learning could not bring about change, if it was not a way of growth, then the university was a waste of time.

Looking back on a lifetime of growth and transformation, coming upon this standstill was a baffling and bewildering impasse. But once seen, it was necessary to find out what it meant and, at the same time, ascertain if it was possible to grow in an educational environment.

Apart from memorization and the integration of facts, I had come upon no real challenge. When trying to figure this out, it occurred to me that the basic structure of the mind was like a computer in which all incoming data had its place; everything fit, and as long as everything fit, no change was possible—thus no challenge.

I realized my particular mentality or basic structure

of mind had been formed long before I came to the university, formed by past experiences and influences, so that much of my thinking, along with values and judgments, was a fairly ingrained response. I all but knew the answers before the questions were asked, because I could predict the answers within the framework of my own mind. Thus all incoming ideas and information were automatically interpreted, adjusted, and incorporated into this preformed structure, and if something did not fit, well, naturally I could not understand it at all. From this I concluded that I did not grow because I had no trouble incorporating new information, and, therefore, the standstill was an intrinsic, not an extrinsic problem. Having realized this much, however, it was necessary to find out how this existing structure could change in order to permit growth, which meant finding the particular challenge that would bring this about.

A well-patterned or preformed mind gives a great sense of security and confidence because it has an answer for everything, and to show how this works, a professor once asked me: what would happen to God if science created life in a test tube? Actually the idea made sense to me; after all, anything we can break down we can build up—the body does it all the time. What would be the difference if we simulated this process outside the body? How would it be a spectacular breakthrough? And how could it possibly prove God did not exist, or that He was not the author of the elements, molecules, or whatever the scientist was putting in his test tube? That the professor thought this could disprove the existence of God amazed me with its naivete and, in turn, the fact that I saw no contradiction in such a proposition amazed the professor. It was obvious we had two different minds, and yet the difficulty he had fitting God into his scientific mind was his particular challenge—his way to growth; whereas I, whether from stupidity or not, could find no challenge wherever I looked.

I had about decided to leave the system when a fellow student told me in glowing terms of a popular professor who was offering a class in the Philosophy of Literature. He was such a favorite, there was a rush to get into his classes, and those who did not make it filled the aisles and sat on window-sills, just to hear him for no credit at all. This turned out to be the most meaningful class I ever took and, from the first introductory remarks, I knew I had found a way forward, found a way out of my private impasse. In so many words, he told us that merely reading the books assigned and filling the requirements would be no challenge in itself; the real challenge, he said, would lie in the ability to step outside our individual frame of reference, our own way of thinking and judging, in order to understand the literary characters in the context of their own frame of reference, or within the context of their own philosophy of life. The first tendency, he said, would be to interpret and judge them in our own light, by our own standards, which would do nothing more than reinforce our own way of thinking; in which case, we would have learned nothing. He warned us, however, that stepping outside our usual way of thinking would not be easy; yet it was the real challenge his class had to offer.

From the outset, I met a mountain of obstacles; obstacles not due to a prejudiced or unwilling mind, but to an unconscious single-mindedness, an automatic habit of judgment I had never noticed before. Initially, I wondered if I would ever be able to step outside my structured mind in order to see into other—perhaps equally structured—minds. Certainly this was a challenge to be reckoned with, and something in me responded with energy.

But this is how a new type of awareness opened up and how it happened that I began the long trek, a trek of many years, to what I call "the open mind" which is a goal, an exercise, a movement that I found continually insightful and enlightening. This was the path through space that I had been looking for, had prayed for. And, as it turned out, what may have begun as an intellectual exercise ended as a medium of grace. Striving for the open mind is vital to the unitive life because it means stepping outside the self and our unconscious habitual ways of thinking and judging. In some respects, it means putting aside the content of personal consciousness, which seems to be a necessary preparation for eventually going beyond the personal or "I" consciousness.

It is well to remember that, consciously or unconsciously, everyone has a personal philosophy of life, a point of view, or frame of reference—whatever we wish to call it. It is according to this we judge, evaluate, choose, and act. Much of our thought and behaviors derives unconsciously and automatically from this mental structure or framework, and until this underlying, preformed structure is brought to light, we can never truly go beyond the self. To step outside an ingrained personal point of view is an exercise in objectivity, a movement away from the subjective self that continually interprets everything according to its own scheme of things, and molds all to itself. The movement toward objectivity is a way of knowing others as they are in themselves, and not as they are in ourselves which, after all, is a totally self-centered way of knowing and an unconscious imposition upon others of our ideas and judgments. These may have reality for us, but they have no reality for anyone else. This exercise made me see how each man's reality is his own, and that the only reality we have in common is the reality we find outside our self, or after each man has stepped outside his purely individual frame of reference. Thus, in striving for objectivity, we are not only going beyond our own way of seeing but, in the long run, everyone's way of seeing. Initially, however, the way out of self is the effort to understand others—to go beyond our self, first of all.

In stepping outside a personal frame of reference, I was made all the more aware of its structure and how, from earliest childhood, my Catholic faith had played a large part in its formation. If in the early years this formation had been largely unconscious, in time it became a conscious choice, an examined way of life. The idea of stepping outside this referent, however, struck me as somewhat risky, for it occurred to me I might possibly lose my faith. But in putting the question to God, in the very movement of doing so, I had my answer. God is already outside my mental structure; He exists without it. He is my deepest existential experience of life, and though I should lose faith in all mental structures, I could not possibly lose God. Indeed, I could no more lose God than I could lose myself and, of course, such a notion at this time was unthinkable, unreal, completely impractical.

But if my knowledge of God derived from experience and not, initially, from mental constructs, it must be admitted there are certain truths of God not always encountered in direct experience. These truths, however, may be avenues of experience, and no contradiction need arise. It is my belief that by living them, religious truths eventually become experiential; meaning, they reach down from the mind to become a living reality to be known experientially, instead of intellectually. I am convinced, however, that should there be a contradiction between experience and truths held solely in the mind, man will go with his experience, because it is his greatest reality. He can sooner deny the contents of his mind than he can deny a profound encounter with God. The history of religion has repeatedly come up against this problem: the mystic is often accused of having "wrong interpretations"—as if it were possible to separate experience from its immediate knowing. An outsider may see in mystical experience an intellectual and experiential variance, but for the mystic, such a separation is impossible, since the nature of his experience *is* the knowing.

But to return to my quandaries, I knew my union with God did not depend on a frame of reference, mental constructs or, for that matter, the Church itself. I decided that if in stepping outside the purely intellectual truths of my faith, these truths proved to have no validity—or were not true in themselves—then I had lost nothing, and would be grateful to be released from anything less than the truth.

Thus, if my Catholic faith could not stand up to an open mind, or withstand such a challenge, then it would go down as nothing more than a good idea, a mere bubble. I always held to the conviction "the truth will out," and that against all odds, sooner or later, the truth would surface, more especially if I had an open mind on it. I felt that ultimate truth was "that" which could never be altered by thinking, was not dependent upon anything outside itself, was indestructible, untouchable—the one sure thing there was. Thus, for me, truth was God; they were identical. Truth defined what He was and, in the end, all things led to this Truth. Thus we cannot possibly lose the truth, and anything less is not worth keeping.

In the long run, as it turned out, all these objections to an open mind were without foundation. In stepping outside a personal frame of reference, I came upon no challenge to the truths of my faith. In my intellectual adventures I never encountered anything that called into question the reality of the Trinity, grace, the Eucharist, and so on. It seems, apart from the theologian, nobody is remotely interested in these truths. Nevertheless it was important to take the risk, to be fearless and willing to give up everything in the pursuit of truth. As I see it, truth in itself can only lie outside the limited, enclosed self, and until we can go outside, all we can have is faith.

But if the fear of losing my faith was short-lived, other problems had to be settled before I could fully accept the challenge of the open mind. One problem was that, after putting aside my standards and principles, I was immediately confronted with a variety of the same—those of other people who saw things so differently it was often difficult to understand where they were coming from. One book on the reading list, for example, was called *The Immoralist,* and I admit the title was initially frightening. It occurred to me that in putting aside my own moral standard I might lose sight of a right conscience, and end up with no conscience or moral standard at all. The solution, I discovered, was to see each case in its own context without imposing my own standards. This does not mean giving up the standards whereby I judge my own actions; it only means giving up the imposition of my standards on others, giving up the expectation that others see things my way and act on my set of principles.

Another question was that, if by seeing into another's philosophy of life I found it superior to my own, what would prevent me from stepping into this way of thinking? If this could happen, I would be back where I started—stuck in a particular frame of reference, which would not represent an open mind, but rather, a mere exchange or substitution of philosophy. It would be like taking off one coat only to put on another. What would be gained in the long run? Better, I decided, to stand free of any coat. But if the ideal is to wear no coat, to espouse no particular point of view, what would prevent me from becoming a dull-witted, spineless character whose mind was a complete void? As I eventually saw it, however, the open mind was not a blank mind; rather it was a mind not stuck in its own subjective perspective, its own views and judgments that are inhibiting to growth; it was a mind that could see other perspectives and alternatives, to thereby gain insight, understanding, and hopefully, wisdom.

As I moved into this new type of awareness I came upon numerous discoveries. The major discovery was the realization of the impossibility of putting on other people's coats—getting under their skin—or having complete understanding of where they were coming from. I eventually saw this as irrelevant and unnecessary; instead, I discovered the true key to the open mind was nothing more than the cessation of judgment itself.

It goes without saying that, when speaking of judgment I do not mean that which is reserved for God alone; rather, I speak of judgment as the glasses through which we see everything, size up people by our standards, for be these good, bad or indifferent, they are judgments nonetheless. The continuous expectation (or judgment) of how things should be, according to our point of view, is a failure to see things as they are, see them as they exist outside ourselves. This type of expectation is a failure to accept others where they are in any given moment, and thereby ignores the reality of change and growth in others—as well as in ourselves. Too often our first meeting with another is our last because, for better or worse, we hold to the initial image and admit of no change. Thus image-making is a judgment itself.

To finally put an end to these unconscious judgments is a form of detachment from our biased opinions and limited ways of seeing. It is an end to putting others down—which is an unconscious way of building ourselves up—and at the same time, it is a recognition of the validity of each individual's view. If we are stuck in our own views, and cannot find a common ground of understanding, then all exchange bogs down in trivia and waste of time. Little children talk either to themselves or at each other, because they are incapable of following the other's line of thought, incapable of seeing the other's point of view; thus little children have no mutual ground of communication apart from physical presence. I once had the opportunity to tape the conversations of young children, and always found them amusing and insightful—a clue to understanding their mentality. But to listen to adults carry on in the same fashion is not amusing; yet it happens all the time—each one talking on his own track. Until we can step outside ourselves, there can never be communication with others or any level of understanding between us, and without this, no relationship is possible, we are no more than physically present to one another.

When we can listen nonjudgmentally to others with a selfless, objective mind, the door opens to an understanding of the ways of God in each soul, which automatically gives rise to charity. Thus the greatest result of the open mind is a charity that knows no prejudice, is beyond the need of mere tolerance, self-sacrifice, patience, beyond a noncommittal silence, and certainly beyond any subtle feeling of self-enlightenment.

This type of objectivity takes us beyond likes and dislikes, and enables us to meet others with an open, clear mind, without preconceived images and with no defensive stance wherein we use our judgment as the standard of measurement for everyone. This allows others the freedom to be themselves and find their own way, without our mentally or silently imposing our way on them. In leaving others free we also become free, and in this mutual freedom there is true relationship and communication. But to give this freedom to others, we must first be secure within ourselves, and the purpose of the unitive life is to give this security, give this necessary freedom.

What seems to be happening here is a gradual emptying of the contents of consciousness. At this time we see how this content has been a helpful crutch, which is no longer needed because it is holding us back. Until now, this content had been the main ingredient, or backbone, of unconscious rationalizations—always used, of course, in defense of our traditional way of thinking—masking a self-protection against possible error, fear of wrong thinking, and much more. At this time we are ready to face all these possibilities, ready, even, to put our whole unitive life on the line.

Earlier in the contemplative journey we learned by experience and revelation that God was beyond all content, but now, having learned this, we are ready to let go of such constructs, ideas, points of view, even as these refer to God. With the secure possession of God, we can now fly because we have no need to hold onto ourselves; we can let go because we are held by God in an irrevocable bond. Thus it appears the interior, experiential self first has to be grounded in union before it is possible to let go the conscious "I," with all its judgments, mental constructs—all contents of consciousness.

Until we come this far, we may not have been aware of how self-consciousness deflects everything back on itself, bends everything its own way; indeed, it is the very nature of the reflexive mechanism of the mind to do this.

But how can we put an end to this unconscious, automatic mechanism? Although the final breakthrough is not in our power, yet we move toward this end when we strive for the open mind. Striving for this objectivity is a difficult movement; it means leaving behind mental constructs and security blankets that, until now, we never knew we had.

Looking at the overall movement of the contemplative life, we can now see that what follows the interior transformation is a further transformation of consciousness—the emptying of all content. This is a subtle movement which eventually lays bare the deep roots of "I-consciousness," and will take us to the fine line or last vestige of the sense of "I." I know of no other path than that of the open mind which leads to this end.

To better understand this phase, we must keep in mind the dualistic setup of the self: self-consciousness above, the unitive center below. Although these are two aspects of the self, they are basically inseparable and continually affect one another; each will have its own particular transforming process. It is only when both transformations are complete that we discover that the unitive self or center was entirely dependent for its existence upon the reflexive mechanism of the mind. In the final transformation, both will go down together.

Though it may begin as a practice and a conscious effort, the open mind gradually becomes a habit of soul; it is the habitual, selfless view of others, of life's circumstances, and even, of ourselves. It happens so progressively we may not be aware that a definitive change is taking place or that, as we grow more objective, we also grow less subjective and, consequently, the self grows increasingly silent.

While going beyond our mental constructs, or emptying the mind of its content, does not imply we have given up the faith, it nevertheless implies we are coming to a point of readiness to see beyond the constructs of belief to the reality itself. Thus a time comes for direct knowledge, a seeing not filtered through a reflexive mechanism, in order to see reality in itself and no longer in "ourself." Mental constructs only point to reality; they help articulate and communicate it just as words communicate thought, yet thoughts are not words and constructs are not reality. So too, in order to come upon truth in itself, we must go beyond the truth in ourself, which cannot be done until we have gone out of self.

At first sight, the open mind may not appear to have reference to the unitive state as outlined by contemplative authors. Yet this particular exercise is nothing more than obedience to the inner prompting of the unitive life itself. After the first transforming process, we become acutely aware of any standstill or lack of interior growth and movement; thus any static state appears incongruous and unacceptable. Without this further movement, we come to a standstill and go no further; we become stuck in the self and the furthest reaches of the contemplative life have passed us by. At the peak of the unitive state, where St. John of the Cross says "here there is no way," I would now substitute the open mind as the way forward, as the unseen path through space. The saint tells us this state is renowned for the full flowering of virtue and for further enlightenment regarding the mysterious ways of God in man and nature; the open mind, I believe, fills these requirements.

This further movement, then, is like the gradual blossoming of a flower that opens in response to the sunlight. It opens upon an understanding and charity that cannot be known when the bud is closed upon itself. This opening-up is a movement of growth into full maturity and beauty of soul, a movement that continues until the petals can expand no more and must fall away. Thus the flower eventually loses itself and, having come full circle, returns to its beginning. This movement away from the center—or away from self—is made possible by virtue of the unitive life—indeed, the full blossoming of virtue has no other end than to bring the self to an end. But once the petals have fallen, this virtue—this interior energy or movement—disappears and the self is no more.

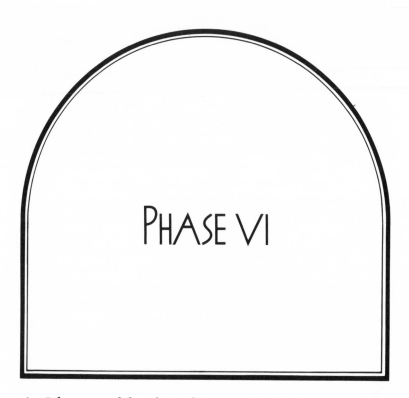

PHASE VI

As I knew and lived it, this was the final stage of the unitive life. It lasted about a year, and on both sides was marked by a definitive milestone. A new state came into being when God lifted a burdensome cross of sixteen years and I walked free and weightless for a period of nine days. This state was similar to the one encountered in the middle of Phase III, in that it was an easy suspension of the faculties that found no obstacle in ordinary routines and, when otherwise not occupied, would sink into a profound absorbing silence.

It was only after the cross had been lifted that I was able to get an objective look at it and see clearly what it had been. Though often labeled as something specific, I now saw its true nature was that of a force going contrary to the unitive life, a force continually trying to break up the unitive bond. As I saw it, this force was the flow of society: its morals, values, judgments, ways of thinking and acting, which I would compare to a gale wind set against a ship at sea, a force moving contrary to the ways of God. Moving against these winds was the exhausting daily burden of keeping the ship in a piece, keeping it afloat. The lifting of the cross was not due to any shift in the winds, however; rather, it was as if the ship had been lifted above the winds to catch a new current. This might be compared to sixteen years of swimming upstream against a torrent, when suddenly the current is reversed and we are caught in a new flow, carried along without effort or opposition. Again, it was as if God had said, "Enough of this, from now on you will be immune to it all," and though remaining in society, surrounded by it, we can no longer be touched by it.

Despite the similarity of this phase to an earlier one, the suspension of the faculties was quite different and, initially, I could not put my finger on how this was so. Later, however, I knew this initial experience had been a foretaste of the state to be: the permanent state of no-self, or the continuous suspension of self-consciousness. Why this suspension did not outlast the nine-day period, or why it did not pass immediately into the further state, I am not sure. But from the events that followed it seems that there was something yet to learn, something more to pass through before no-self could become a permanent reality.

In my journals at this time, there is increasing mention of the experience of loss-of-self, a loss on all levels but one—the final loss of all sense of self-awareness, which I was afraid would result in a complete blackout. It never occurred to me that beyond self-consciousness was a new type of knowing, and that my fears were without foundation. When I searched through contemplative literature for evidence of a permanent loss of self-consciousness, I met with disappointment. Though I knew contemplative states were not referred to as "changes of consciousness," yet in terms of mystical theology I knew this would have to do with a permanent suspension of the higher faculties of soul—the reflective memory in particular, since without a memory we cannot possibly remember ourselves. Thus I was looking for an account of a permanent suspension, a permanent state of full union, or prayer-of-union. But, as noted earlier, St. John of the Cross affirms that this can never be a permanent condition in this life. According to him, full suspension is only temporary; it is but a passing transient experience. Looking back now, I find this inexplicable, inaccurate, and unacceptable.

But apart from the suspension of the faculties, another way to define the falling-away of self-consciousness is in terms of entering a permanent state of contemplation—contemplation being the fixed gaze upon the Unknown, which St. Thomas Aquinas says is the highest state of all. Later, I would call this gaze "the Eye seeing itself," which is how I define God's "knowing."

While mystical theology is concerned with this fixed gaze—which is as much of the beatific vision as one can sustain in this life—it is evidently not concerned with its consequences—no self. And if the theologian is leaving this to the psychologist to explain, he is making a mistake, because psychologists know nothing about it and say nothing about it; I do not think they even admit the possibility. Those involved in formulating mystical theology need to do much work in this area, because understanding the result of a *permanent* suspension of the faculties is far more crucial than any understanding we have of the dark nights.

I might add that we must also include in this permanent suspension the faculty of will, which we thought had long ago gone down to God when we first came into the unitive state. It seems that there is a further disappearance of the will, a will no longer united or one with God, a will that disappears entirely. With the close-down of self-consciousness, the unitive will disappears, and in its place is an immovable silence, wherein there is no longer any sense of personal energy or personal will. Nothing at all.

Without knowing it, this phase was the immediate preparation for a radical change of consciousness. Due to the nature of the experiences, there was the intuition of something ahead, something greater than anything encountered before, a glimpse of a state never thought possible in this life. There was a sense of impending change, of grace, of the nearness of revelation and, as I often thought, a getting ready for a great explosion.

Apart from increasing experiences of loss-of-self there was another factor that marked this stage. The steady, interior flame suddenly flared up to become a burning torch, burning at great intensity. I referred to this as the "thermostat," and sometimes prayed to have it turned down, then up—there were many regulatory complaints, yet none of it was under my control. But for all the wonderful heat generated by this thermostat, it had unusual repercussions, because this is where I came upon certain extraordinary problems.

Prior to this time, the interior power or energy at the center had remained stable; it was the indistinguishable aspect of self and God. Though often under stress from outside forces, this center never moved, the flame never wavered; it was a bulwark of steel and a powerhouse unto itself. Because I had no power to express this flame to the outside, because I could not use it or tap into it, I came to think of it as belonging to God alone. In turn, however, I could not distinguish my own deepest energy from God's energy, and therefore could not distinguish the true self from God. Nevertheless, I was continually trying to figure out where "I" left off and God began, or what exactly was His and what exactly was mine.

Matters stood this way for twenty years, when suddenly, in this phase, there was a movement in the center, deep inexplicable rumblings which gave me the idea of an impending explosion. When the thermostat was turned up, there came with it an energy never encountered before, a problematic energy in that it gave rise to a rash of extraordinary experiences, such as mind over matter, levitation, out-of-the-body experiences, foreknowledge, knowledge of others, and even the possibility of healing. Whatever the true nature of these energies, it was obvious they wanted to reach to the outside and find expression. I felt about to be used as a medium for these powers, and what this meant, I had no idea.

From earliest years I had no attraction for the extraordinary and placed no value on such things; in fact, when still young I referred to visions and voices as "cheap spirituality," because it relied on appearances and was without depth. It had nothing to do with God, not, at least, as I knew Him. Although the present experiences did not include visions and voices, they may have touched on everything else, and were very disturbing; disturbing not because I placed no value on them—I could always change my mind in this matter—but because they were so foreign as to be impossible to incorporate into the self I knew. To superimpose the extraordinary on the life of a most ordinary individual is a mistake; it does not fit. I did not know how to behave or what to think. If, from the beginning, I had been led by an extraordinary path, I would have taken this in stride, but as it stood, these experiences were disturbing, and totally unnatural. I wanted to be rid of them, rid of the energies that gave rise to all these phenomena.

For several months I observed and studied these mysterious energies and powers, trying to understand their purpose and find the true source. Because they arose from the center, I knew they belonged either to God or to myself—there was no one else around, nothing inside but the two of us; thus the source had to be one or the other. If from God, I felt it should be acceptable to me, fit like a glove, be natural. On the other hand, even if from God, its passage through the self to the outside was enough to taint its purity, and thus it was the self that was unacceptable, either way I looked at it. It seemed to me that a true medium should be selfless so that God's grace could flow through, pure and unfiltered. But if the self steps aside, then where is the medium? In such a case God would have no medium but the empty form; I could not see how this would work.

The only thing I knew for certain was that these energies were admixed with some unknown aspect of the self, and their disturbing feature was their sudden, unexpected, spontaneous uprising—their unpredictableness. To have this type of interior power over which you have no control is frightening, for even if harmless and benign in its movements, there was always the possibility that things could get out of hand, become outlandish and ridiculous—which they did. There was the fear of eventually becoming a puppet to those powers, and if this happened, I would lose myself.

Now it is one thing to lose your self in the great silence, or in the suspension of the faculties, but quite another to be squeezed out and overrun by some unknown power. I felt this latter form of loss-of-self carried with it the possibility of insanity, and nobody wants to go that way. As it stood, I never knew what would happen next, and when you do not know, you learn not to trust yourself, and when you cannot trust yourself, the situation becomes unbearable. What is more, I could find nothing particularly spiritual about these phenomena; though I learned a few things—which I shall recount later—there was no increase of depth or enlightenment, love or virtue; I felt it taught me nothing about God, and had much to do with externals, other people, and the superficial.

My conclusion was that if, after all these years, God wanted to make me a medium or give me some mission, He would first have to make it acceptable—make it fit in with my life and personality and, above all, give me the certitude that this was His doing. I figured that, if truly from God, I would never be able to get rid of these powers, but if from some disguised aspect of the self, then nothing would be lost in getting rid of them. Thus the test was whether I could get rid of them or not. I might add that this was a very old test I had discovered early in life—namely, the conviction that it was possible to be rid of everything but the truth. We could be rid of thoughts and experiences, rid of every space we were caught up in, and yet the truth would move with us; whatever could be left behind, then, was not the truth. I will not go into how I discovered this acid test for truth, or how it proved itself again and again; I will only say it was a way of discerning what was from God and what was from the self. Because it never failed in the past, I was sure it would not fail me now.

But how to get rid of something not under our control seems an impossible task. Ignoring and giving these powers no value is not sufficient strategy to be rid of them, since they come and go as they please anyway. I began to observe, to watch and see if I could get their time of day or circumstance, find some clue to their occurrences. I noticed how energy was generated during hours of interior silence—prayer, Mass, alone in nature—how it had a tendency to spring alive when other people were around, which was always disastrous. Although not sure of the exact nature of these energies, I could not wait till all the answers were in; by that time it might be too late. Thus I devised a plan for their extinction, which, in a nutshell, was to starve them, give them no inlet or outlet—snuff them out like a flame without oxygen.

This meant giving up prayer, giving up the ability to sink into the center, giving up my whole spiritual life, in fact. It meant giving up writing in my journal, because this was an outlet; giving up talking to others, because I never knew what I might say; giving up taking walks, because in the beauty of nature I might get carried away. In a word, this was the regime of an extreme recluse. I had no idea how long it would take, but was convinced that sooner or later, without an outlet, these energies would have to give up—die out.

From the start, I can compare this difficult regime to sitting on a volcano or riding a bronco. When you put a lid on boiling water the pressure builds the more; the lid suppresses nothing. But the great mystery was the determined resolution to do this; where did it come from? If this was my own energy, then what energy was putting down another energy? Actually there was no other energy, there was only conscious determination.

The first week was unforgettably terrible; the interior energies were practically coming out my ears. But almost from the beginning I thought I noticed a slight waning, a subtle diminishing of power, and with this I took hope. After the first week, I knew I was on the right path, because the decline was steady and surprisingly rapid. In less than two weeks I could resume a more sociable life-style and go back to prayer. Then, just as suddenly as they had appeared, these energies disappeared, and in their wake was a peace and silence greater than anything encountered before. It was then that I saw the irony of the situation. It struck me forcibly. I had undertaken this battle in the effort to preserve my self, to keep these energies from running over me and getting out of hand, but in putting them down I had unwittingly put down the self. Thus, in trying to preserve the self I lost the self. This was an amazing discovery. How clever and ingenious the ways of God!

Later I saw how this works. I saw the self as a dual set-up; one self, but two aspects. The interior self is a powerhouse of energy and movement, and can be an object to the mind, but the conscious self has no such power of movement, yet it is privy to a knowledge higher than anything that can be experienced by the interior self.

Thus it was the conscious self and its knowledge, its intuition, that put an end to the energy self, which illustrates how knowledge is more powerful than power itself.

Ordinarily the division between self as an interior energy and self as a self-conscious mechanism, or type of consciousness, is not noticeable; it does not arise in the unified state because the sense of wholeness is such that consciousness and the energy center are in complete agreement, working as an undivided unit. But with the uprising at the center, this division becomes apparent—and disturbing.

As long as we are able to integrate or incorporate the extraordinary, we would not be aware that this division in the self exists. This would be the case of saints and mystics who were led this particular way from the beginning, and took the extraordinary in stride as nothing unusual or divisive. For myself, of course, this was not the case. Yet for me it proved to be an important disturbance, because in putting down this interior energy, I was unknowingly getting ready to live without any interior energy; for in the state of no-self there is nothing left that could be called interior energy. This does not mean that all interior energy is from the self. Once the self is put down, the burning flame remains, but it is an energy we cannot claim as our own, thus only God can put out this flame. And He does.

I think of this flame as that which never exceeds the mean—never gets out of hand or causes any great disturbance. Yet when this divine thermostat is turned up, some unknown energies of the self come with it, indicating that, all this time, God has been keeping these energies in line, keeping them from exceeding the mean. But now He is releasing them in order to throw them out, get rid of them entirely, so His great plan can go forward. To come upon no-self, there must be none of these energies left.

It should be remembered that in putting down the energies of self, we are not putting down something evil, bad, selfish, and all the rest; this is not the impassioned, self-centered ego. These energies are harmless and benign, yet they waylay and deceive us; they are an impasse in that they cannot be pure mediums of God. In fact, I am not sure the self can be a medium at all. Putting away these energies is nothing more than an unmasking of the self.

Too often we think extraordinary phenomena are a gift from God when, more often, it is only the self masking as God, the self insuring its survival under a divine guise. Coming to this final phase of the unitive life, the uprising of the self is like Custer's last stand—just one more battle before the final defeat, one last effort to gain control. Unconsciously, the self knows it is about to be snuffed out, and this is its final play for divinity. In putting down these energies, we unknowingly deal a death-blow to the self, and thereby open the door to complete loss-of-self. Evidently, dealing with these energies is a major and final hurdle to overcome before no-self can become a reality.

After twenty years of not being able to distinguish in the deep energy center what was mine from what was His, when the thermostat was turned up, this discernment could now be made. Although God is the ultimate source of all energy, the self has a tendency to misuse it for its own ignorant purposes. In the unitive state, I believe God keeps these energies in hand; we do not even know we have them. But in the preparation for going beyond the self, these must be released so we can deal with them, see through them, unmask them, and have no doubts about it.

About this unmasking, what is worth noting is the method of discernment. The energies were deemed inappropriate for the simple and obvious reason that they did not fit naturally, they were incongruous with the personality because they could not be incorporated into the known self. I regard the personality or known self as something superficial, nothing other than a front to the world. When totally immersed in silence, where is the personality? Without people and the external world, there is no such thing. Personality only exists in our relationship to others, and has much to do with how others see and reflect us, or how we see and reflect others. This is why we feel more at home with ourselves when alone, or in silence and solitude. Few people realize that a great change takes place after spending time alone, and the longer the period of time, the greater the change. Only by being alone can we become aware of the superficialities in our relations with others, because we now see the difference between the unknown, which we are, and the known, which we are not. We also see that the known is the personality, which we are not.

But this is why the disruption of the unknown self at the center is equally disrupting to the known self and why the known acts as the discerning partner of the unknown. Had there been no disruption of the personality, these energies and extraordinary experiences would have had to be incorporated somewhere in the past, or more gradually, perhaps. As said before, this would be the case with those who travel the extraordinary path from the beginning. It would also be the reason why the extraordinary saints and mystics did not go on to tell us about the state of no-self, which lies beyond all such energies and experiences. These energies run contrary to the great silence of God, and contrary to a permanent loss-of-self. To get caught up in them is to be locked in our house and never go beyond its narrow confines.

When these experiences came to a peaceful, silent end, it was only a few months before the end of this phase. Before proceeding, however, I would pause to say something of what I learned from the experiences themselves. Not all were from the same source; not all were from the center. One experience in particular was insightful; it was what might be called an out-of-the-body experience. Strictly speaking, the term out-of-the-body is not accurate, because the fact is that we are never out of the body. What the label tells us, however, is that we can be aware of a division within ourselves and this awareness is more accurately called out-of-the-body. There are several types of these experiences; for myself there were two.

The experience in which I learned nothing profound was seeing myself either lying down or walking around, which was a miserable state of affairs because I did not know which I was really doing—it was that real. But as this was happening, I noticed a switch in my brain that I interpreted as the switch that determines either the sleep or waking state—depending which way it is tripped—and that somehow I was on top of the switch and could not get off. I would say to myself: I am going to get up and get out of this state, and then I would get up and walk around—seemingly, that is, because, in truth, I never got up at all. Yet I had the feeling of getting up and walking around, and then became aware of myself lying down; I would wake up and say: this time I am really going to get up. Then I felt myself getting up and walking around, which was not the truth. This went on and on; it was a miserable state. But the switch was interesting; I all but saw it moving back and forth, and wondered how in heaven's name I could keep it in one position. This state interested me because it was not a waking state, not a sleep state, and not a dream state—it was just a switch, that's all.

This experience reinforced my view of the brain as a series of switches, and that we have a switch for just about everything. As a child, I noticed my mind had increasing levels of silence, and that I could not always get to the deeper levels. When I could go, however, it seemed as if some door opened to let me in, as if the mind had many doors, many switches, just for silence. Sleep is an entirely different switch from mental silence. In fact, when we fall asleep, it is the end of mental silence, the end of the contemplative sphere. We do not have to be long into the contemplative life to realize that sleep forfeits true silence, because true silence belongs entirely to the waking state.

There is, however, what might be called an "in-between state," which we are tempted to think lies between sleep and wakefulness; this is not the case. If, in this in-between state, we fall asleep, immediately there is an end of the state, an end of silence. This in-between state really is the borderline between two different levels of silence; it is not the borderline between sleep and wakefulness. The in-between state is actually the gateway to complete mental silence, complete suspension of the faculties. As I remember it, this state is most apparent toward the end of the transforming process. When the process is over, or after spiritual marriage, this phenomenon disappears, and only the great silence, a complete waking state, remains.

But the out-of-the-body experience I found insightful was of another type altogether. I do not know what triggers this experience, but some unknown aspect of being—let us call it "spirit," and not "soul" or "psyche"—rises above or moves out a distance from the body; in this movement the spirit gets all the bliss, and the body gets all the thoughts and feelings. What pulls the spirit back into the body and ruins the bliss is self-consciousness. As soon as I reflected on myself—my thoughts and feelings—and allowed myself to become conscious of the division, the experience came to an end. Right here I understood that some form of consciousness—which I later realized was self-consciousness—was the link between these two aspects of self or being, and that it would be impossible to maintain the blissful, free state as long as I reflected on myself. The irony was that as soon as the division dissolved and I sank back into the body or feeling self, I was whole again, one without division; I now realized this was an inferior state of affairs. Thus in this division I saw a state far greater than that of unity or wholeness.

This experience was actually a giant leap ahead; it was a true experience of the completed state of no-self. At the same time, this is not how we get to no-self; in fact we cannot get there by ourselves at all. There was no way I could create this division, much less sustain it; it is a very gradual process, a journey in itself. At the time, of course, I did not know this; I had never heard of no-self. Indeed, if it had not been for the sustained suspension of the faculties and impending loss of self-awareness, I would not have thought of self at all.

But even if I could not make it happen, I nevertheless learned something from this experience. I could see that by not reflecting—looking inward, paying attention to thoughts and feelings—one could live in a blissful free state; yet it appeared we would have to be out of the body to do so. I went on, however, to discover that this was incorrect; we do not have to be out of the body to realize this state. The bondage of spirit is not the body; rather, it is a type of consciousness—self-consciousness—that creates an apparent division. What makes for a sense of unity is this division. Thus when self-consciousness falls away, no such division exists, and therefore no unity exists. Without this consciousness, the spirit is no longer hampered by the body, and there results a sense of formlessness, a certain lack of body awareness—even though the body remains. This means that the true division in man is not between body and spirit, but between two different states of seeing—the difference between self and no-self. Thus the body constitutes no obstacle for realizing higher states.

It is a surprise to realize we can have the beatific vision while in the body. But if we think about it, this makes sense. If God is with us here and now, then where do we go when we die? Do we really go someplace to see God? In the tomb, did Christ go someplace? I think we know the answer to these questions. We do not have to travel to outer space or be out of the body to see God; yet we must make a journey of sorts in order to span the gap between two ways of "seeing," to see God without the division created by self-consciousness.

There is a certain irony in the fact that we cannot be aware of this type of division until we first attain the wholeness of the unitive state, and that we cannot go beyond the unitive state until we are aware of this division. It seems to be a circular journey of sorts. The truth, however, is that the contemplative journey is a spiral movement in that we come back to where we were, only now we are a step up from where we began. Thus life is one of constant repetition, only on higher and higher levels—or deeper levels, depending on how we look at it. St. John of the Cross, for example, talks about three dark nights, each one different, and what we call betrothal and marriage are also repetition on different levels. There are cycles of darkness and light, disruption and peace, even death and resurrection. Old mental and psychological structures are being broken up to let in the new, which is gradually incorporated into ordinary life. What is changing is not the ordinary round of life, but the different levels of living it, seeing into it.

Because it is a spiral movement, there is a great deal of misinterpretation going on; that is, one level of experience is interpreted or seen in the light of another level—usually a lower one—which is invalid, of course. Theology, too, has levels of intepretation, yet few people reach the higher levels because they are afraid to let go the lower ones; they cling to the low levels like babies to their bottles. But we can see how various levels of interpretation have given rise to untold confusion in contemplative circles, errors that have gone on for centuries. It is imperative to break out of these circles by recognizing the true, spiral movement of the interior life.

A final note on division has to do with the experience of levitation. Here the spirit is not yet free of the body, and therefore takes the body with it in its upward flight. Levitation reveals no division—it also reveals no purpose—yet it may be the prelude to realizing a higher division. Once the spirit is free from the limitations of form, there is no levitation, because the acclimation to a sense of formlessness is complete; thus—to put it crudely—the spirit is no longer knocking into the body.

I think there are different types of levitation or experiences of it; the only one I knew was a sudden, swooping thrust from the center, much like St. Teresa's flight-of-the-spirit. Her experience of levitation, however, was different. For at least a year before this experience I was able, in my sleep, to lift off any time I wanted, for the mechanism seemed to be under my control. In the waking state, however, it was a very different experience, and never under personal control. In the waking state it is more spiritual, although I admit it had an odd way of coming to a dead end. But then, I am convinced all extraordinary experiences lead to a dead end.

A beautiful experience, however, which stems from the center, is the ability to contact the center of other things. It was as if my center ran into the individual center of everything else. To contact the center of another person is the rare experience of knowing God in another in such a way that there is no central difference between self and other. To contact the center of an animal is to contact love—indeed, to contact the center of anything is the experience of love, even when the object is inanimate. Where a type of mind-over-matter may be involved is when, contacting the center of the inanimate, there is the possibility of substituting centers so that our center causes the movement of something else. When I came upon this center business, I thought of St. John of the Cross's statement of how all things have a center, and his suggestion that God is the true center of all that exists. I believe this completely. Man is not the only one who has a center or whose center is God.

Contacting these centers is actually the prelude to a different way of experiencing God in all things. If we could put these centers together, we would glimpse the reality of how all emanates from God and how it can be said: God *is* all things. But for now, this is purely a unitive experience because, later, the unitive center gives way— explodes—to reveal that God is neither center nor circumference, but All.

Altogether these experiences were of short duration; I make no claim to expertise in these matters. In some experiences, self was the source, in others, self was an obstacle to a higher grace. But one way or another, the true nature of self was being disclosed and unmasked, and this, I believe, was the sole purpose of these experiences.

In the lives of saints and mystics extraordinary experiences are well-documented; it seems they are likely to appear at any time in the contemplative journey. They were known in the blackest of nights and the brightest of illuminations; thus they are not state-bound or indicative of any particular stage.

St. John of the Cross, of course, would have us throw them out whenever they occur. His attitude was that they could lead to deception, and the truth of God was better known in interior silence. St. Teresa, on the other hand, notes that these experiences came to an end, or were greatly lessened, at the time of spiritual marriage. From her biographies, however, we know that, despite the lessening, she was subject to these experiences to the end of her life. But then, she traveled this way from the beginning of her "conversion," or during the last eighteen years of her life. Also, her experiences were of an entirely different nature than those we have been describing. The disruption I speak of has nothing in common with her sixth mansion, or that period prior to the realization of her goal of union. Nevertheless, I can see from this and my own past experiences that a disruption always occurs before we move to a higher level; it is the breaking up of the status quo, an opening to the new, and a letting go of the old ways which have outworn their use. Every disruption portends the onset of another circular movement up the spiral. This is the true nature of every dark night and every disruption at the center. It is all a period of preparation.

Toward the end of this phase, or after the mysterious energies had disappeared, there remained the burning flame, the love which I now clearly saw was not mine. I understood this selfless love belonged to God alone; it was His love for Himself, or Christ's love for the Father. But if Christ was all that remained of the self, if it was he, not I, that loved the Father, then where was I? How was I needed anymore? When I could not answer these questions, I began to feel lost and wrote about this unusual predicament. At one point I asked:

1. *How much of me can be united to God and still walk around?*

2. *How much of me can actually become God?*

3. *Where do I let off and where does God begin?*

4. *I intuit that some part of me is so one with God that a part of me is lost to myself. What part is lost and what part remains? After God throws us out to fill us with Himself, what are we to do with our thrown-out selves? What need does He have of us anymore? In me, He loves Himself; I don't count, I feel unnecessary to*

creation. He came, He conquered, I am no more. I don't understand this. I think he should take not just a part of me, but all . . .

—Journal, *1978.*

From this point forward the silence became so great, so pervasive, that the end of the last vestige of self-awareness seemed but a hair's breadth away. Still, there remained the subtle fear that, when the last vestige disappeared, the result would be complete unconsciousness, a complete blackout. I did not know that, where self-consciousness ends, a new consciousness begins, a new state that opens upon a whole new life. Despite all the glimpses and foretastes, despite the preparation of a lifetime, there was nothing to indicate the reality of this further state.

One time, in a very intense experience, I was given to understand that, from now on, God would be loving Himself not *in* me, but *in* Himself, and I had no idea what this meant. As I saw it, my true self, or Christ, was already in God, so already God was loving Himself in Himself. It never dawned on me there was another way of understanding: that all things were so immersed *in* God that nothing can be separated out and, therefore, nothing has any separate existence of its own—no separate individual being—no separate "I" *in* which God dwells. Later I saw how this worked; I understood that God is *in* things only because all things are *in* Him, and thus with God on the inside and God on the outside, God is a flow-through, flowing freely through all that exists; and even "that" which He flows through is part of the great flow. Self puts up a barrier to this flow-through of God; it stands, as it were, between God on the inside and God on the outside. But once the self disappears, one of the first things we "see" or experience is the Great Flow, and how all things are truly in God, not separate, and that God is no longer *in* the self—nor is He the self.

But it was only after the journey beyond self that I had full understanding of what it meant: God loving Himself *in* Himself and no longer *in* me. It meant God would no longer be loved as object or *my* true self, which is the way He is known and loved as long as He is *in* me, or as long as "I" remain. But when there is no self, He is loved *in* Himself—pure subjectivity, not *in* any thing.

The "I am," self, or self-consciousness—whatever we care to call it—can only know and experience God as object (or center). We know God subjectively in ourselves as part and parcel of our being. He is our greatest subjective experience; thus we know God as well as we know ourselves, and in a nondualistic way. Yet the truth remains: we only know ourselves as objects to an unknown subject—unknown because as subjects of consciousness we cannot see the "I" (or observer) directly; we cannot look into our own eyes. So too, we do not know God as subject as long as the subjective and objective poles of self-consciousness remain. But what would it be like to know God *as* subject, outside or totally apart from the self? Who can imagine what this is like? In truth, we cannot imagine it. Thus, if we know God on the inside as subjective experience, He is *still* the objective pole of self-consciousness, and matters will remain this way so long as any self remains. To know God purely in Himself, and with no self, takes a new type of "seeing" and a radical change of consciousness. Until we come upon this change, we cannot understand what it means: God loving Himself *in* Himself and not in "ourself."

Here we might point out St. Paul's experience, "No longer I, but Christ lives in me," as typifing the unitive state, where the words "in me" attest to a sense of interiority as well as a sense of self—or "me." If, on the other hand, he had said, "No longer I, but Christ lives," such a statement suggests a different meaning, wherein the "I" or "me" has dissolved and all that remains is Christ, indicating a state beyond union and beyond self-consciousness.

There is a tendency to think that God ceases to be an object of consciousness when the imagination or image forming mechanism of the mind closes down, or when the cloud of unknowing descends. Though this is a step in the right direction, wherein God reveals Himself on a profound subjective level, even here God is a formless "object" of interior consciousness. In fact, just the ability to look inward indicates a reflective consciousness, and tells us the conscious "I" remains intact. In other words, simple awareness of our center belongs totally to a self-conscious state because the nature of this state is such that subject and object, or "awareness *of*," can never be separated. Many people, of course, think these poles can be separated; Hindu psychology seems to hold to this belief. Still, as long as any reflective ability, or looking inward, remains, no true separation has occurred. It goes without saying that, when either the subjective or objective pole of self-consciousness disappears, both poles disappear together, in which case there could be nothing left to call a self.

This means that the unitive state is a nondual, subjective experience (below the neck) within a dual type of consciousness—the observing "I" (above the neck). If we can understand this, we have some idea of the radical transformation that is needed to take us beyond the unitive state.

But, getting back to the state of readiness, I intuited that it was only a matter of time, a short step, before complete loss of self-awareness became a reality. The pull to spend more and more time in silent prayer increased tremendously and, initially, it was only at such times that this loss appeared imminent. It was only after finally passing over the divide that the Great Silence became the whole of life, every second, all day—forever. Then the feat is the ability to sustain the silence while walking around, doing all the ordinary things. It comes with time.

Despite the intuition of being on the brink of a final surrender, there remained subtle fears of what would happen if I passed over the divide and never returned. To pass over for a little while would be fine, but to pass over forever . . . I could not imagine it. Though God encouraged this surrender, I did not know how to cooperate; just wanting to give our all does not make it happen. We give this and that, but nothing changes; then suddenly God takes what we never knew we had to give, and everything changes. It seems only God can bring about real change because only He knows how to do this, only He knows when we are ready, or how to proceed thereafter.

Evidently, still wanting was the ability to wait in the great silence without fear arising; if there is fear of never coming out of the silence again, God will let us have it—have the self back, that is. Trust in God is so vital that everything hinges on it; our whole past life with God is brought to bear on this moment—do we really trust Him with our life? Can we dare to abandon all? Are we ready to surrender every last thing we could ever call a self? Like St. Peter, perhaps, we jump up and respond: yes, of course we can! But when we see the cross of self-extinction down the road, we turn and skip town.

Passing over the great divide is one point in our contemplative journey where God does not force the issue; we are not pushed out of the plane. Rather, we will not know the moment we are out. No-self does not come about by traumatic means. We are not taken by force or overwhelmed, we are not possessed by a power, there will be no fear of self-annihilation; we do not know the moment it happens except in retrospect. All we know is a common, ordinary silence; it is when we try to move out of this silence and discover we cannot do so, that we realize we have passed over. Acclimating to this silence is what I have called a journey, a journey beyond the self.

Before passing over the divide, however, I experienced one more upheaval in the center, a battle of such gigantic proportions it was beyond me already. I stood looking on as an outside observer, a bewildered observer, and for the first time asked myself: Who or what is watching this? The battle was incomprehensible and, no doubt, by reason that it was beyond me, it did not touch the self. Rather, it lay deep below the feelings and outside the mind. Thus it evoked no response; I was only aware of its distracting presence. My impression was of a battle taking place between two unknown forces, forces that had nothing to do with me, and what they were fighting about or how it would all end, I had no idea.

Nevertheless, as possible explanations I listed six ideas in my journal, which I then found unconvincing, and thereafter resigned myself to not knowing. In retrospect, however, I was given some understanding of this battle; but before saying what I learned, I will first mention one of the six explanations because it proved to have significance.

I thought perhaps Christ was angry with me. As childish as it sounds, within the context of my life this notion had much validity. For one reason or another, Christ and I had been doing battle from the time I was eleven years of age. No sooner did we call a truce than it would start all over again. This battle is virtually the story of my Christian life, the only life I have ever known.

Just before the onset of the interior battle, I had a tirade against, not the Church—which I regard as mystical—but against those in the Church who exploit Christ by using him as a weapon of self-righteousness; who use him as a sword of personal defense to put down others and puff themselves up, because they are so blind that they cannot see what they are doing. These are the narrow-minded hypocrites who claim they love the Church, yet unwittingly kill the spirit in the name of Christ, who keep more people out of the Church than they let in because they lack openness themselves. I told Christ I saw charity running out of his church like a mighty river and if he did not dam it up, it would soon be an empty reservoir, good for nothing. I told him to round up all the hypocrites and herd them over a cliff, because if we were supposed to go to the Father through him and his church, then we were being asked to crawl through a brood of vipers, an impossible requirement. Either he would have to clean up the church or step aside so we could get to the Father without him. If we could not go through him, then we would have to go around him—go to the Father without him.

I do not remember what sparked this tirade; no doubt it was the build-up of years and years that spewed forth with the uprising energies already mentioned. If all I had to do was walk out of the Church and slam the door, it would have been an easy matter, but the fact is that I had done this before and it didn't work. But the tragedy lies in the fact that Christ cannot step aside; he is a fact of God, the truth, and for better or worse, this is the way things are. To ask him to step aside is like asking God to kindly drop dead. It is like the dirty window image again—we cannot see through it because it is covered over. This is a poor analogy for Christ, yet it illustrates the peculiar impasse others have created for him. We cannot see through him to the great reality; he has been covered over by layers and layers of thought, concepts, intellectual interpretations, dogmas, theology, narrow minds, and on and on. I have often thought if, after Christ's death, we had only passed around the four Gospels and never said another word about him, the whole world would be Christian by this time. There is no use going into how this would have worked; it is too late now. We have been raised with interpretations that are probably glued forever to our mental structure, so that to know the reality of Christ would take a gigantic miracle, a frightful unhinging for which few people are prepared.

But we can see how the tragedy of Christ is linked to the tragedy of the church, in that few people see below the surface of either. But the moment one of us sees below the surface, then it becomes our personal tragedy as well. In an obscure way, I knew this tragedy most of my life; for me, the sight of the cross was a sight of some unknown, tragic impasse to the full realization of God. It would be many years before I looked at the cross to see how the deepest, most profound tragedy shades into pure bliss, and that the outstretched arms of dire abandonment are also the outstretched arms of bliss. Thus there comes the time when tragedy is bliss, or when Christ, despite the tragic impasse, gives way to reveal his clear identity. What this means is that bliss awaits those who can possibly make it through the tragedy of what has happened to Christ in the Church.

After this tirade, the interior battle began and, putting two and two together I thought to myself: Christ is mad at me again. Although this explanation did not fit, I later saw it had not been entirely inappropriate. The battle lasted two days; on the third day it disappeared, and a few days later the self also disappeared. What disappeared was the true self, the Christ self; to return to the Father, this self has to step aside, be relinquished, given up. It is this surrender of the Christ-self that makes the journey of the cross so bewildering and awesome; yet it is the only loss that makes possible the journey to the resurrection. But just as Christ lost his divine self on the cross, we too must lose the Christ-self in order to return to the Father. Thus Christ does battle all over again against those forces that would prohibit this transition, prohibit this journey beyond the self. That I never had to do battle for myself—it did not touch me—is the marvel of such a transition; from here on the burden of death and resurrection is on Christ. He alone returns to the Father, and how this takes place is the unfolding revelation of the journey itself. The self does not take this journey, because everything we can call a self vanishes, and "that" which remains is only revealed at the end.

Another explanation I listed had to do with Job, who thought God was angry with him—it seems he could find no other explanation for his predicament. It is the nature of man to think when things go wrong, he has fallen out of favor with God, or that God is against him. He reasons this way because he does not understand the ways of God, which is another way of saying: he refuses to accept his own lack of understanding. To think we understand the ways of God is akin to satanic deceit—the apple of divine knowledge. We deceive ourselves when we believe that the kind of knowledge we have (the self-conscious type) is the kind of knowledge God has. The truth is: our way of knowing is not God's way of knowing, and the closest we can approach God's knowing is by full, total acceptance of unknowing, or by not knowing. This does not mean we walk around in a stupor; it means we let things happen to us—accept them without question. Once I saw the pride of wanting to know God's ways, or of understanding what was going on in my soul, I stopped questioning, and resolved to carry this battle around for as long as God saw fit. But the battle was short-lived; on the morning of the third day I wrote:

O blessed reprieve! After communion this morning the faculties slept peacefully without threat of interruption or distraction. All was still, all was nothingness, no joy, no love, and no self. I felt out of myself, but not in an ecstatic or "held" way; but rather as if my soul were asleep. I did not want to move, wake up, come back to myself. This can hardly be called an experience, yet it may be the greatest yet. In describing it I say "I exist," but this does not fit. To say all my faculties have been totally humbled is a good explanation, but it does not tell the whole story. To say "I" no longer exist is the nearest to the truth I can come to expressing it. It left me physically weak and interiorly numb; it is an effort just to write this—to reflect back and try to understand, yet the experience taught me something:

1. God has had mercy on me. I could not produce this state myself. I did not feel His hand, but intuited it was His work beyond a doubt.

2. In this sleep I failed to exist but did not question how, why, or what for. All was so still I gave myself up to becoming nothing and in so doing, knew it was the right thing to do. This taught me that only in total self-forgetfulness, total lack of self-awareness, could I ever hope to enter into the ways of God. All my questions to Him, all the debates, all striving to understand, avail nothing. I saw that Job finally came upon the right answer when told we do God an injustice when we question anything. So too, I learned not to question, not to strive to understand—and did I not suffer for this knowledge; was I not punished just for wanting it? Is not the great sin wanting to know God's ways?

3. I know I must not trust my analysis concerning what I feel or experience. I could be mistaken and use incorrect labels all along. In other words, I may not know myself after all, much less comprehend God's ways in my soul. I must never again presume to understand the way He leads me or His purposes.

All that is not total surrender and abandonment is pain. We ourselves cannot surrender or abandon our self to God. He must take us of his own accord and in his own time. He alone can accomplish this total surrender—we cannot even do this much! To question God is to incur suffering. To try and understand His ways is suffering. To try to reach Him of our own accord is suffering.

—Journal, *1978.*

This was an important lesson to learn. The ability to accept and not question is imperative for taking the journey beyond self, because we will be entering a new way of knowing in which the old way becomes meaningless. Self-consciousness and its particular way of knowing disappears, and the great silence, the great unknowing becomes all; thus, once we are in the Great Flow, our usual anchors will not hold anymore.

Before entering the flow, however, I had insight into the true nature of the interior battle. I understood the two forces as self-preservation and self-extinction, over which man has no control—though he thinks he does—because God alone has the final say. It would seem these forces are ordinarily living in balance and, when an imbalance occurs, self-preservation (keeping the self intact) rises to the surface—to the rescue. Some people believe self-preservation is man's deepest instinct, and that all behaviors can be traced to it; this, of course, is a lopsided view. It is understandable, however, that no one wants to deal with self-extinction; it is too frightening, we put it down as abnormal, and give it no place in the true scheme of things. But if properly understood, self-extinction is man's ultimate salvation; otherwise, we would be stuck in ourselves for all eternity and never see God, who is beyond the self. This would be hell.

From the age of five I had a number of experiences of self-extinction ("threats," as some might call it) and, though I had no understanding of what this meant, I knew it had nothing to do with physical death. These experiences always had to do with God; they were frightening revelations, which somehow I thought would put an end to me. What was amazing, however, was that, despite the fear of extinction, it never happened. I was not annihilated, swamped, or overpowered; I did not black out, become a robot or a stupid puppet, I did not go out of my mind, or go to hell—or whatever the fears that self-extinction can evoke. The final extinction is not like this;

it does not happen this way. In fact, when it happens we only know it in retrospect, as a *fait accompli*. It is just that quiet, silent, gentle, and unspectacular. God is not a looming power, but total, absolute silence. One of the reasons we do not know when it happens is that, without self-consciousness, we immediately lose our usual way of knowing. Thus all our self-conscious fears and expectations come to naught; they have no place when another way of knowing opens up.

Acclimating to another way of knowing is the journey that lies ahead. (Full adjustment to this took me three years.) And just as self is the true state of self-consciousness, so, too, is no-self the true state of no-self-consciousness. It goes without saying that, when we pass the divide, the two forces of preservation and extinction evaporate. Without a self, these forces have no meaning and no place. There will be no more interior battles; indeed, there will be no more "interior" at all—no awareness of a "within."

A week after the battle ended, I wrote:

Oh God, guide my pen that I might tell of Your workings and doings in this soul. This morning, so gently as to be imperceptible, total silence came over the faculties; I felt nothing, no presence, no joy, only a kind of staring. To move physically was so difficult and painful I dared not move at all. There were certain physical fears about getting to communion—but I made it.

The next step is total unconsciousness and the very thought of it is frightening, please God it will never happen. I want to give myself up to God totally without fear, but when God would have His way in a soul He does not take external circumstances into consideration, nor am I out of the body sufficiently not to care or to be aware of where I am or what I should be doing— that's the next step. But when and if it comes, I won't know where I am so, I won't care or even be aware. In other words, there is still some degree of self-consciousness left. I am aware of where I am and that I exist in a body. That I am B is totally irrelevant, but that there is a soul here in which God finds a home is too good to be true. God has taken possession of it and at the same time this causes me no ecstasy or joy, because I do not feel it is my own soul, but rather His soul. I cannot believe God would take joy in the funky, small, almost sinful soul of B. He is too big for that—it can't be. But somehow, by His taking possession, a soul is transformed, enlarged and purified so as to contain Him. I am no longer keeper of the house; in fact, I may not touch it, cannot praise or thank Him for it, because it is not my house anymore, but His. Perhaps it never really was mine; all I know is that I once thought it was, and now my perspective has changed; I do not belong to myself anymore, I belong to Him—in Him, with Him, for Him—Him!

I wish I could explain all this better. I want to say two things:

1. The experience—written down somewhere—of Christ living in me and no longer myself, that is the clue to what I experienced today.

2. What has happened is more than a union of wills, more than silence and peace; it is the total union of the faculties wherein I am only capable of attending to the present moment. No thought ahead or behind. To keep in this state I seem to need only remind myself of what I am doing . I say to myself: now I am driving, now I am shopping, now I am writing, etc. My mind seems incapable of wandering. To wander is fruitless and unnecessary, and to force the mind is a sin. So as long as I lose myself in the present moment, all is well; but to think of the past or future is like kicking against the goad and causes unnecessary suffering.

I wish I could talk to somebody about all this . . . but such is not given to me."

—Journal, *1978.*

A few days later occurred the experience which begins *The Experience of No Self,* wherein self passes over the line and is never seen again.

This brings us to the end of this book and, as I lived it, the end of the unitive life. Initially, I thought no-self to be a further state of union, but after the entire unitive center disappeared, all notion of this being a unitive state fell by the wayside. However hard we try to justify union without a unitive center, it cannot be done.

When the unitive life falls away, however, we do not suddenly become God; God does not suddenly disappear. All that happens is that we finally take our rightful place with Christ in the Trinity as part and parcel of God—God manifest. The ultimate realization of no-self is not its identity with Father or Holy Spirit—the omniscient unmanifested Father or the omnipotent manifesting Spirit—rather, it is the realization of our true nature, our true identity as the manifest aspect of the Trinity—Christ. In this breakthrough, we also realize the Oneness of Christ, Father and Spirit, three distinct, non-interchangeable aspects of the Godhead. There are no such things as greater or lesser aspects of God; the three act as one, and to finally see how this works is what no-self is all about.

The unitive state runs into the state of no-self; it is the means by which we come to it, and if these pages have given any insight into how this happens, they will have accomplished their purpose. This final phase of the unitive life is not well defined in contemplative literature, yet it is there. I have seen it again and again, but for some reason, it fizzles out, seems to go nowhere; I can only speculate about why this is so. For myself, this phase was a tremendous preparation, yet I never expected what was about to happen; in some ways it seems not to be in the preparation itself. It was only in retrospect that I was able to look back and see this phase for what it was—a getting ready. For what it is worth, I will end this personal story of the unitive life with a recapitulation of the final stage.

By a merciful stroke of God, the cross of many years was lifted, thereby freeing me to enter more deeply into the unitive state. I immediately encountered a silence of the faculties different from anything known before, and more pervasive. The outstanding feature of this silence was the impending loss of all self-awareness, a loss I had never thought of before, had never sought or looked for, a loss I never expected and had never even heard of. This possibility was something new. It was utterly bewildering.

At the same time, the usual steadily burning flame suddenly rose to become a torch of great intensity. This was not my own love of God; it was too great for that. Rather, I saw clearly that it was Christ's love for the Father. But when this thermostat was turned up, there rose with it other unknown and unwanted energies that gave rise to a rash of unusual experiences. Lest these experiences get out of hand, lest I lose myself to these energies, I decided to put them down. But in putting them down, I unwittingly put down the self—thus to save the self, I lost the self.

Although the unusual experiences lasted a short time, they served a learning purpose. In the main, they disclosed a division between self as an interior energy and self as a self-conscious mechanism of the mind—both of which will soon be lost. When the interior energies disappeared, there remained only an intense silence in which God's love for Himself was all. I began to wonder where I fit in, or how I was needed anymore, and went through a period of feeling lost. Though I knew the last vestige of self-consciousness must be surrendered, there was the fear of what would happen then; also, I did not know how to bring about this surrender. It seems we must wait upon God's own time. Only He can take away the self, take us over the great divide; only He knows the moment.

When passing over the line was imminent, there was a final interior battle between two unknown forces that, mysteriously, did not touch or involve me in any way. Later I understood these forces as self-preservation and self-extinction, over which no man has the final say. After two days these forces disappeared, leaving a great interior silence; the center was absolutely still. A few days later, self-consciousness entered this silence and no-self became a permanent reality; a new life opened up. Acclimating to this new life is a journey, a new movement in the contemplative life. I see this journey as the final trek to the resurrection, and a recapitulation of Christ's experiences; that is, what he realized after he gave up his self on the cross.

After all our battles, I never dreamt of going this far with Christ, but that it happened is all thanks to him. Because he would not step aside or let me go around him, I had to go through him, and now, having discovered what it is possible to realize on the other side, I pray he will continue to be a stumbling block to all who try to bypass him. I pray he may continue to do battle with all who search for the truth, and in this battle I pray: let the best man win and the worst man lose!

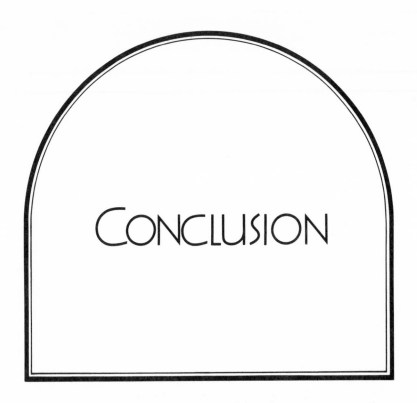

CONCLUSION

This writing has been prompted by the conviction that we have long been mistaken about the true nature of the unitive life, and due to this misunderstanding the state has become all but unrecognizable. It is my belief that contemplatives have been thrown off course and misled, to the extent that there may be many living in this state who have no clear recognition of such a reality. The remaining pages will address this subject, give the reasons for this belief, and say something about how these misunderstandings have arisen.

It is imperative to see the unitive state in the context of man's overall development—a development I regard as entirely spiritual in nature—and realize it as the state in which God intended man to live his most productive years, or when he takes on the challenges, risks, and responsibilities of life's burdens in the full exercise of his unitive selfhood. St. John of the Cross refers to the unitive state as Adam's original state, or the state in which man was intended to live. Here man walks with God, relies on His continued companionship, is one with His will, and accepts his humanity and all that this entails.

In society as a whole, few men reach this state, and therefore earthly life is anything but a paradise. Thus the challenges to the new Adam will arise from an imperfect society going contrary to God's will and original design—and, consequently, to Adam in his unitive state. After this, however, the analogy between Adam and man in the unitive state falls apart, because Christ revealed to us a higher destiny than Adam's union with God. Christ lived his entire life in Adam's original, unitive, sinless state, yet he went on to suffer, die, and be resurrected. Thus he takes us further than Adam, and reveals that our ultimate return to the Father is far more than the return to Adam's original unitive state.

Nevertheless, before we can reach our final destiny with Christ, we must first return to our original unity with God; when we do, we have reached a midpoint in our total spiritual development. In other words, to go beyond the self, we must first realize the self in its oneness with God, because in the exercise of this unitive self lies the mechanism of transcending the self, of going beyond it to realize Christ's final destiny. Union first, then death and resurrection. This was the way Christ showed us; this was the movement of his life.

It is important to point out that the unity we have been discussing has little, if anything, in common with Western psychology's notion of personal wholeness, or with the process of individuation, integration, self-realization, and all the rest. The truth is: Western psychology has never tapped into the contemplative dimension, and the notion that it has, has misled us regarding the true nature of the unitive life. Psychology has tried to heal the split in man, heal the man divided against himself; where it has accomplished this healing, we have nothing more than the unity of man with himself. This is completely different from the unity realized by the Christian contemplative, for whom unity with himself is a byproduct of his union with God. This distinction is important, because mere unity with one's self (the union of the conscious and the unconscious which Jung called "mystical union") will never enable man to transcend his self, since there is no built-in mechanism for doing so. Only union with God has the vital mechanism for transcending the self, because only God can make this a reality; otherwise, going beyond the self is sheer insanity. On this point, Western psychology is correct.

Actually, psychology stops at the self and admits of nothing beyond. In the case of any loss of self, the analyst would expect the psyche to be overrun and invaded by the demonic forces of the unconscious—which evidently lie in wait to carry us off to hell. All I can say about this fairy tale is that whatever forces could possibly exist outside God (naturally, I do not believe in such forces), the contemplative has learned from the beginning to face whatever comes; with God as his security, he runs from nothing. Few people realize the invincible position of the soul that walks with God; there can be no overestimating the marvel and splendor of such a position. With God, in God, for God—this is a power unto itself.

Nothing reveals the inadequacy of Western psychology so much as the popularity of the Eastern religions in the West. Obviously, these religions are offering a dimension not available in our Western scheme of things. Where Christianity has compromised itself to go along with Western psychology, or has tried to translate it into spiritual terms—symbolic tokenism, I call it—it too, has failed us, because it stops at the self, and thereby forfeits its true Christian contemplative and mystical dimension. For this dimension to go forward, Christianity must leave Western psychology behind, because this psychology merely scratches at the surface. Christ showed us the way; this is all we need to follow.

Everyman's first goal is to realize his oneness with God—this goal is the same for everyone across the board, contemplative and non-contemplative; in this, the contemplative goal is no different from that of any other Christian. But the contemplative differs in his calling to go further, to go all the way with Christ—to die and to rise, all in the short span of this life on earth. This is why union with God is, for the contemplative, but a midway point, and not his final goal. For ages past, contemplatives have been mistaken when they took for the end that which is only a beginning—if you will, Adam's own beginning.

The transforming process of the contemplative journey—otherwise known as "transforming union"—is God's intervention in the soul's ordinary spiritual process of maturation. Here God accomplishes in a short time what otherwise is accomplished over a longer period. The obvious purpose of this accelerated movement is to realize more quickly the full unitive state, in order to move on to the final emptying of self—to go through Christ's own experience of death and resurrection. This is why the calling to the contemplative life is the greatest of human destinies, and why half-measures are the greatest of human tragedies.

We cannot compare God's intervention in the night-of-the-spirit with any Western scheme of psychology, and we look in vain if we try to find it there. When I first heard of the psychological process of transformation, I became interested, and wanted to find out if it had anything in common with the contemplative experience that goes by the same name. As far as I knew, Carl Jung had the most to say about this process, and therefore I undertook the task of reading all his books in print. As one who never had a mind for mythology, symbolism, dreams, or wishful interpretations, I found these books tedious and boring, yet I persisted in the hope of eventually finding some breakthrough into the contemplative dimension. Unfortunately, it was not to be found; these works are devoid of the contemplative experience. In fact, I found nothing there that was even comparable to it. Evidently, Jung never tapped into these depths, and therefore could not have recognized it in others. In a word, he does not address himself to the Christian contemplative community. Some of his followers, however, have tried to reconcile and translate his scheme of the psyche to fit the contemplative dimension. But this is worse than if no attempt had been made at all, since it has only given rise to confusion that has waylaid and misled many.

For certain individuals, perhaps, Jung's notions may be insightful and helpful, but he sheds no light on the experiential dimension of the contemplative, and errors made in good faith, but with insufficient light, must not be perpetuated. At any rate, this psychology has been a major source of our failing to understand the true nature of the Christian unitive life; the contemplative has been thrown off course when told that the realization of the self is the end of the journey. This is not his final goal at all.

Let us make clear that we have been speaking of three different transforming processes: (1) the union of man with himself, (2) the union of man with God, (3) the accelerated contemplative process of union with God. It will be helpful to keep these distinctions in mind for all times, since the failure to do so has been the cause of much confusion.

Within the accelerated movement, there is a further distinction between the extraordinary and ordinary transforming process. As we know, the extraordinary is accompanied by visions and voices, ecstasies, raptures, and so on. I have always thought of this as the path of the mystic, and obviously it has not been the concern of this book. Nevertheless, because the extraordinary has been set up as the gauge and shining example for the ordinary, this, too, is a major source of misunderstanding regarding the true nature of the unitive life. Where, for the mystics, the unitive goal is realized in a flourish of high excitement and experience, the ordinary contemplative realizes this same goal in the silent, still waters deep within. I have always found it difficult to reconcile the extraordinary with the true depths of the contemplative movement. These depths are not clearly defined in the extraordinary experience, because the deeper aspects are overshadowed by the vision, the sensory business, and the superficial message. Nevertheless, these experiences are everlastingly held up to us by contemplative authors, and taken as the sole authority regarding the experience of union. In this, we have all been brainwashed.

As soon as we focus on the extraordinary, or the transient and superficial, we miss the essential, substantial, lasting effects of the unitive life; we miss its depths and forfeit its reality, we virtually trade it in for illusion and wishful thinking. Yet we do not even know we are doing this, because we have been so utterly misled. We wait for what never happens and look in the wrong direction; we gauge our experience by others', use their criteria for our own and, altogether, have been so badly thrown off course that we no longer recognize the true unitive life, cannot discern it in ourselves.

The type of understanding we derive from reading the lives of others is primarily intellectual and imaginative, secondhand. But the type of understanding we come by within ourselves is wordless, thoughtless, imageless. And between these two types of understanding is the same gap that lies between fiction and reality. There is no bridging this gap; one can never be the other. Yet how many would rather live in the mental "space" of fiction than have to face, day after day, the mundane, trite, often boring reality of ourselves? It is because we choose the fictional space that we have been brainwashed and thereby locked out of the true reality of the unitive state. In truth, the unitive life is utterly real, common, ordinary, and unspectacular; it may even be boring. It is not easy living.

Reading the lives of saints and mystics may have its place in our lives—though it would be better if we had never read them—but a million times more important is our awareness of every interior movement and change, even the most subtle, because this is where it is *at*, this is where the Spirit is continually moving us, transforming and informing us in its own particular way. This is where we will learn everything we ever need to know, and to do this, we must clear our minds of everything else. When we come to believe that the unitive state is only as saints and others have lived and described it, then we have blinded ourselves to its subjective reality and settled down to a world of make-believe. Let us take an example in point.

In the lives of the saints, mystical marriage is described as an unusual, overwhelming experience, one that marks the entrance into the full unitive life. This experience is obviously transient; basically, however, it is the realization or "seeing" of a profound interior union that has already been established, a union revealed by the dark night in the chrysalis. The realization is new, but the union is not; in fact, for some time we may have intuited or obscurely known of this union, but now, in the experience of mystical marriage, it has come to full light. We see clearly and without doubt that we have "arrived," or that the butterfly is complete. Only afterward, in the exercise of its new life, does the butterfly gradually realize it has been locked in (the marital aspect), and that without an ego-center, it can no longer do its own will or merely go its own way. A life of selfless giving is not a matter of personal choice; rather, selfless giving will be the very wings of the butterfly that propel it through space. Doubt enters when we read of mystical marriage in the lives of mystics, and can find nothing comparable in our own lives. Somehow the mystics always manage to cast doubt on our personal experiences, which, by contrast, seem so ordinary, unspectacular, and practical. But let us be wary of this. Let our experience speak for our self in the same way that the mystic's experience speaks for his self. In other words, we must not let the mystic speak for us; we must not let his experiences become the gauge of our interior life. When this happens, we may wait indefinitely for mystical marriage* or other milestones that have already passed us by, or wait for spectacular signs that may never come at all. Christ was right when he said that those who need signs lack faith, and contemplatives are not always up to the mark in this matter.

But if, in its deepest aspect, mystical marriage has nothing to do with a transient, self-gratifying experience, we have been further misled by authors who give the impression that, once the soul enters the full unitive state, it becomes a charismatic being who goes forth to set the world on fire, or act as a light to all who are fortunate enough to draw near. This is not even the way it went with Christ. There is nothing about the unitive state that guarantees automatic recognition from others.

All that is attained in the unitive state is the ability to live our lives as God originally intended—that is, in oneness and partnership with Him. Any other view is blowing it out of proportion, making it into something it was never intended to be, making it a final goal instead of a midway point. Altogether, this distortion has made the true unitive state unrecognizable. Indeed, we have worshipped the golden calf instead of fixing our gaze on the mountain where He appears.

---

* The term "mystical marriage" should be eliminated from contemplative terminology because, for most of us, it belies the reality of this turning point, which is not a moment of union, but the full, experiential *realization* of this union.

It would be interesting to take a poll of Christian contemplatives around the world to see what they have to say about the unitive state, to find out how they see it—and how many are in it. This survey would best be limited to those who have given their all to this intense pursuit for at least ten years. Actually, from the beginning of one's conversion—used in the Teresian sense as that point in life when we throw everything out but God—six or seven years is all we really need. Here I think of Elizabeth of the Trinity and other young souls, but since we must include the likes of St. Teresa in this poll, we have to stretch it to ten years—at least.

Such a poll would provide us with the opportunity to gather valuable information regarding the interior life—there are many questions we would like answered. And as for the study of mystical theology, the responses to such a questionnaire would be more revealing than anything we have learned so far in the field. This would give us the opportunity to concern ourselves with what is going on with contemplatives today, to stop comparing ourselves with what went on hundreds of years ago. For our immediate purpose, however, I would ask the following three questions:

1. How many have been through a period roughly equivalent to the night of the spirit, or entered the painful cloud of unknowing, or had a deep shattering experience from which they eventually emerged with a new, deeper, more subjective, non-intellectual knowledge of God?

2. How many have come upon the abiding certitude or awareness that, in the depth of their being, or interior center, they are one with God?

3. How many have experienced mystical marriage in the way described by St. Teresa, St. Bernard, or other mystics?

Putting aside any hope for unanimity among contemplatives, I would nevertheless expect the majority to answer "yes" to the first two questions and "no" to the third. If correct, it means the majority are in the unitive state and know they are. When the response is positive for the first question and negative for the second, here arises our concern for a better understanding of the unitive life, especially how, in substance and essence, it is utterly simple and unspectacular. From those who hold to the notion that union is a rare achievement, or only attained on the deathbed, we will naturally find "no" on all counts, and this would strike me as sad indeed. Such a negative view reminds me of what a Buddhist once told me. He said the ultimate Buddhist goal was only attainable after one had lived many lives—like 10,000 or more. I said, "Oh, for God's sake, if I really believed that, I'd never bother to make a beginning!" Indeed, I would not have begun the contemplative journey if I thought extended time were involved. Since I fully expected to die young, it had to be a quick passage.

There seems to be something immediate about Christianity, something the Eastern religions do not have. The belief in rebirth is an obvious retardant, and no doubt a ruse of the self to insure its survival through death after death. In some ways, this illustrates that, without union with God, we can never get rid of self, never go beyond it; indeed, how can self get rid of self? And, too, if God does not remain when self is gone, then what does?

But if every Christian is called from the beginning to realize union with God, how much faster should the contemplative travel who, by definition, has been given a special calling, a special destiny, and a special grace. I find it incredible that anyone believes that realization of union is the rare experience of a few privileged. Christ's message and grace is not for a handful of rare specimens; yet contemplative authors and authors on mysticism perpetuate this false impression. Let us beware of these misleading notions and call a halt to them whenever we can.

Another problem we may have in recognizing the unitive state is that, when the preparation is right, this state will fit like a glove and seem perfectly natural. As they came from the hand of God, did Adam and Eve feel perfectly natural or perfectly supernatural? Actually, we only know one by the other, because all knowledge is relative or relational. But this is why the supernatural effects of union can only be known in the *exercise* of the unitive state (and not merely in the unitive state itself)—or when the going gets tough. Even then, it becomes natural to us, which is why the trials have to become tougher and tougher—as they usually do. It is in the very testing of this indissoluble bond that the self is dying while, imperceptibly, God is filling the empty space.

We must realize that when awareness of union becomes a habit, we lose its active consciousness, because the habit has become incorporated into our everyday functioning. When we first learn to drive or solve a math problem, we are absorbed in our task, totally conscious of every detail, and always checking on ourselves. But over a period of time, we do the same things and never think about them. Yet whenever we please, we can deliberately reflect on these skills, because they are permanent facts of our life. This analogy is apropos to the unitive life.

After finding our true center, we become increasingly conscious of its existence, we explore and experience it thoroughly—which may take years—and then settle down to living and acting from the center until the time we know of no other way of living, or until it becomes an ordinary, unconscious way of life. Still, we can deliberately reflect on this unitive center anytime we please—and we do this often. This means that if we lived all the time in the state of supernatural bliss, we would soon acclimate to it, find it a completely ordinary way of life, and, possibly, even find it boring, and begin looking around for something else. I am convinced that this is the way it goes for all eternity, because there is no end of God, no end of the continuously new, for as soon as we acclimate to one state we start to move on.

Because the unitive state becomes an unconscious habitual way of life, we need continuous challenges and trials to bring it to the forefront of consciousness. And the greater the trials, the greater the awareness of the unitive strength and its sense of deep imperturbability and joy. Somewhere St. John of the Cross refers to the unitive state as a bag of spices that has to be shaken up periodically in order to be enjoyed—to enjoy its reality and its presence, which otherwise lies within as merely a potential. In part, this bag of spices is the virtues or qualities of the unitive center, and unless we are virtually shaken up now and then, they lie dormant, and the true effects of the unitive state cannot be known. In time, therefore, we discover that union with God as part and parcel of our being is the most natural thing in the world; we were made for it; this is the way God intended us to live from the beginning. Nevertheless, the naturalness of the unitive state will, for some, make it less recognizable.

It is important to separate or distinguish those experiences that belong to the cocoon stage—or to the emerging butterfly—from those unitive experiences that belong to the mature butterfly who has long since been through the transforming process. The experiences of the emerging butterfly are what we usually hear about in glowing description, because after this, the experiences are not so spectacular. If, as soon as we emerge, we write up these transforming experiences, publish them, and hand out the good news, we are only generating premature excitement based on the newness of the state. It is all misleading, because without distance, we mistake the part for the whole. Let us hear instead from those who have lived twenty to fifty years in this state, and we may hear a different story; now something will have to be said about "what happened next." We need to hear about this, we need to hear about the ordinary life of a mature butterfly. Usually, it is rather boring.

I knew a priest who was in the unitive state. He had been through the night of the spirit, but after all the wonderful experiences, he came upon a certain let-down, and seemed to have a difficult time reconciling himself to the utter "ordinariness" of the state. For this reason he was bewildered and humbled, he felt perhaps he had lost something, that somehow he still had a long way to go— but go where? He took for granted that he had not been given the graces of the saints; in a word, he had about him the air of humble disappointment. Though he had the unitive secret deep within, he otherwise had a poor image of himself. I always remember him as the most humble man I ever met. I was very young at the time—he was the only spiritual father I ever had—and, for a while, I too wondered what had gone wrong. But many years later I realized that in this priest I had met the living reality of the unitive life in all its simplicity, humility, humor, discernment, depth . . . when I think of it, he was "ordinary"—but extraordinarily so.

The sense of a falling-off or of encountering a "wasteland" that sometimes occurs after emerging from the cocoon, is actually the butterfly leaving the chrysalis behind as it flies into the unknown where "there is no path." It is the onset of a life of selfless giving and yet a further stage of death to the self. This is where the contemplative may feel lost and wonder what has happened to all his former experiences, and wonder, too, if something has not gone wrong. Also he may still be waiting for the experiences of the saints, and possibly a share in their renown. From here on, the glory of the unitive life can only be known in its fearless exercise, which means the full acceptance of our humanity and selfhood. Here we must literally lay ourselves and our unitive life on the line, as if daring the forces of hell to separate us from God. This alone is the way forward to the final emptying, to the loss of everything that can be called a self.

I hope my references to the "exercise" of the unitive state have not been construed to mean that we become rebels, daredevils or anything unusual, or that this exercise is thought to be restricted to any particular way of life, monastic or otherwise. Wherever we are, whatever we do, God will see we are tried to the limits, and have every opportunity to exercise the unitive life.

So far we have seen how a misunderstanding of the true nature of the unitive life has arisen from a number of sources. For one, we failed to understand it as a midway point in our spiritual development, as the full blossoming of selfhood, the unitive Christ-self, which leads to final loss of self, and Christ's death and resurrection. For another, we have been misled when gauging our unitive expectations by the extraordinary experiences of saints and mystics, and thereby have overlooked the substantial and essential for the superficial and transient. We have been equally misled by modern psychology, which regards self as the ultimate realization of man; misled in that it has never tapped into the true contemplative dimension and knows nothing about it. We have been misled by failing to recognize that the life of the butterfly is natural and ordinary, because the unitive state is the true state in which God intended every man to live. And finally, we have been misled by failing to see that, built into the courageous exercise of the unitive life, is the mechanism of the self's death in God, and that with this death another transition begins.

In summary, the unitive life is the true state of selfhood, of man living his life with God, giving his all to Him, accepting all from Him, totally one with His will. In the exercise of the unitive state—the exercise of selfhood—the self is dying, being consumed, worn down, used up, forever unable to put itself first before God or other men. It gives generously and courageously because of its interior security, because of its invincible bond with God in the deepest center of being.

Finally the time comes when the soul is asked to surrender the last vestige of self-consciousness, and go beyond all that could be called self. When the self enters the Great Silence, another transformation or acclimating process begins, and this is where we begin the transition from death to resurrection. We do not go beyond the self because it is worthless, self-centered, and of no value. On the contrary, this self is God-given and, for a time, is part of our humanity, it serves a great purpose. Yet self as an interior energy and a self-conscious way of knowing stands in the way of pure vision, and therefore must ultimately be relinquished.

What Christ went through on the cross and in the tomb was not the Dark Night of the Spirit; his purpose was not to realize union with God. Christ's death and resurrection was of an entirely different nature. What Christ gave up on the cross was his divine self, his oneness with God as it was known through the same self-consciousness mechanism he shared with us all. Because the nature of human consciousness can only know God as object, this was the way Christ, too, knew God: the Father without, the Spirit within. As the vessel containing the Spirit, Christ stands midway between the two, and thereby reveals to us the Trinitarian nature of God. But if, at the incarnation, Christ took on our way of knowing—God as object—at his death he returned to his original way of knowing, the indescribable knowing inherent in the Godhead of absolute Oneness.

As I see it, the contemplative's destiny is to be so totally transformed into Christ that he can say: only Christ dies, only Christ rises. Christ alone can span the void beyond object and subject; this is his return journey to the Godhead, which he repeatedly makes for each one of us. It is a journey beyond self and the unitive life, wherein the unitive bond dissolves to reveal that its underlying reality is the Trinitarian bond between Father, Son, and Spirit. Thus union ultimately gives way to the greater reality of the Trinity—the Oneness of the Godhead.